GOLF

CROWOOD SPORTS GUIDES

GOLF

TECHNIQUE • TACTICS • TRAINING

Bill Brampton

Edited by Alistair Tait

The Crowood Press

First published in 1991 by
The Crowood Press Ltd
Ramsbury, Marlborough
Wiltshire SN8 2HR

British Library Cataloguing in Publication Data

Brampton, Bill
   Golf: technique, tactics, training
   1. Golf. Techniques
   I. Title   II. Tait, Alistair
   796.3523

ISBN 1 85223 604 3

Dedication
To Leslie King – one of the greatest and most influential golf teachers of his generation.

Acknowledgements
Photos by Matthew Harris. Illustrations by Graham Gaches.

Throughout this book, the pronouns 'he', 'him' and 'his' have been used inclusively and are intended to apply to both males and females.

Typeset by Chippendale Type Ltd., Otley, West Yorkshire.
Printed in Hong Kong by South China Printing Co.

CONTENTS

PREFACE

Golf is a wonderful, inspiring and fascinating game. It is unique in its infinite variety of challenges. You can play it alone or with a partner, or fight out a contest against a field of competitors.

Its handicap scoring system also allows you to play on equal terms against anyone in the world. But be warned – once you get into golf your life will change. All of a sudden, the time you couldn't spare for other endeavours is found to play a round of golf, and this process could take anything up to five hours. What other game offers players with ambition a realistic chance to become a millionaire? All you have to do (and I don't say this lightly) is to acquire sufficient skill to average seventy strokes around a championship course in tournament conditions and nothing and nobody can stop you joining the millionaires' club: what a prospect!

Realistically, though, what are your chances of joining this select club? For instance how difficult is golf to play? It is incredibly difficult at the highest level. For example, when you watch touring professionals performing in a tournament, you are witnessing a performance that is equal in skill to a concert pianist displaying his talents on a concert platform. The average person would never expect to emulate the concert pianist, but many believe that they could join their idols on the stage of professional golf without too much effort.

For an amateur to play a round of golf in par is a superb achievement in itself! The odds of the high handicap player producing such a score are extremely remote. Even touring pros find it hard to match par, and they are at it day in and day out. Just observe how many are actually under par for each round. You will be surprised how few make it.

The temptation remains, however, for amateurs to join the professional ranks, yet during the past ten years only one amateur champion has made a successful transition to the pro ranks and that was a Spaniard: the gifted Jose Maria Olazabal. The rest have either re-instated as amateurs or are struggling at the wrong end of the Order of Merit.

Why? To my mind the answer is patently clear: the majority of swings that work in amateur golf simply do not convert to the professional scene because they are badly shaped, usually too long, too wristy and far too physical. To the uninitiated, their swings may look impressive and stylish but to the trained critical eye they contain too many variations and compensations. If the player wishes to be consistent under the demanding conditions of the tour grind, then his action and swing shape must be solid, reliable and settled, otherwise he has no chance.

We shall be looking at a compact action in this book, developed around what I term a good shape or outline. I shall be exlaining later how and why this will work for you, no matter what your aspirations.

Most importantly, the system contains an important option in that it allows you to get as good as you want to be without having later to re-think your game should you wish to convert to the professional ranks.

This, of course, is preferable to living in a fool's paradise with an amateur-shaped swing, never mind having to make major changes while trying to earn a living on the circuit. That scene is littered with such casualties.

Only one man in recent times has managed to make a successful swing change while still on the tour, Britain's Nick Faldo. He had the courage and determination to go through that awful period during which the old habits refuse to lay down, sure in the knowledge that he was replacing them with good ones. Even now Faldo lives with his coach in his hip pocket. Few in the world could afford that luxury. Imagine what a force Faldo would have been had his 'new' swing shape been with him at the start of his career. . .

My plan in this book is to lead you through the tangled mass of different swings, to advise you on which parts you should copy, which you should ignore and why, so that you build one simple, solid, effortless swing. I shall also be giving you positive instruction with unique exercises to help you to develop the skills inherent in world class players. In the mean time, we will get an insight into the mysteries of the game itself.

Fig 1   Nick Faldo's change of swing shape made him a world class player.

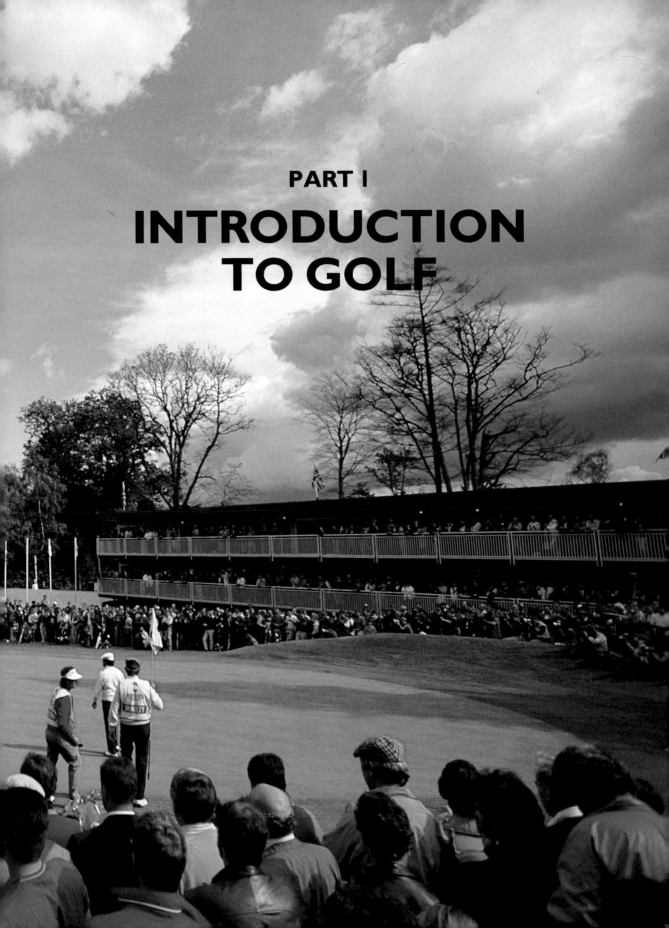

PART I
INTRODUCTION TO GOLF

CHAPTER I

WATCH ONLY GOOD PLAYERS

When you first go out into the wide world of the local municipal golf course, you are likely to see some horrific sights. Gone are the smooth sweet swings that perhaps inspired you when you watched golf on TV. Instead, you will witness golf as it was meant not to be played. You will see things such as bad posture, and golf balls pulverised in every direction, left, right, high and low – many will even be ferociously driven into the ground. People who play in this fashion are termed 'hackers'. Occasionally, the law of averages will allow a bad swipe to produce a straight shot. I term this the 'roulette syndrome': every swing is different, and it is only sheer chance that produces a winning hit.

Avert your gaze from these sights if at all possible and concentrate on what you are trying to do. Do not be sidetracked into often trotted out advice such as 'head down, stiff left arm and eye on the ball'. This advice doesn't, and won't, work.

The moral here is to avoid watching bad golfers. Humans learn by imitation. This is a well known fact, so make a vow to go to as many professional tournaments as possible. Do not waste time trudging round the course. Take your lunchbox to the practice area and stay there. Drink in the rhythm, ease and economy of movement that produces good golf shots. Compare what you see with the recommendations in this book, remembering that all swings seem different. Then seek the ones that look the nearest to our model and copy them. Copy particularly the short iron swing, keeping it economic, crisp, well balanced and on line.

You may still see a few extravagant swings, so use your new knowledge to define which is best to imitate. In that way,

Fig 2   Jose Maria Olazabal – one golfer who made a highly successful transition to the professional ranks.

good habits are formed and become instinctive. Remember that!

If you can't get to many tournaments, then offer to caddy for the low, single-figure men at the local club. Watch how they swing, not how the 'hackers' hit.

How about watching golf on TV? I regret that not a lot can be learned from a two-dimensional image, and the cameras too frequently concentrate on the putting surface. The technical comments on the golf swing are, at best, repetitions of well worn clichés which are mostly unintelligible to the beginner, and aggravating to

competent golfers and those involved in teaching. There is no substitute for the three-dimensional image of a world class golfer at work on the practice area.

Sam Snead is one great champion who learned from watching. He caddied for good players, copied the best he saw and had an illustrious career, becoming a legend in his own lifetime.

In years to come I am sure holograms will become a reality as a teaching aid. In the mean time, find time to watch the good players in the flesh, particularly on the tournament stage.

CHAPTER 2

THE OBJECT

The objective of the game of golf is simple: to strike a dimpled ball 1.68in (4cm) in diameter with an implement called a golf club a predetermined distance into a hole in the ground, which hole is approximately 4in (10cm) in diameter.

The ball is played from a teeing area to a green where the hole is indicated by a flag. The distances between teeing area and green vary from as little as 90yd (80m) to more than 600yd (550m). Between these distances there are various areas. The bigger expanse is the fairway.

The Fairway

This is a mown area of grass and can vary in width from 20yd (18m) up to and beyond 50yd (45m). Its length also varies. On some easy courses, it can stretch from tee to green, but this is an exception.

At the perimeters of the fairway, the grass is allowed to grow a little longer and this is called 'semi-rough'. Beyond this, the grass grows unchecked and can be interspersed with heather, ferns, small bushes, etc. In other words, it is unmanicured terrain, hence the term 'rough'. Besides the rough, natural ditches, small ponds and even lakes will be left in strategic places. Bunkers, or sand-traps as they are known in the USA, are constructed along the fairway and around the green to punish wayward shots. The complete playing area is termed a 'hole'.

The Golf Course

A golf course usually consists of eighteen holes but some short courses only have nine (see Fig 3). Each hole presents a unique challenge, requiring you to get from tee to green in a defined number of

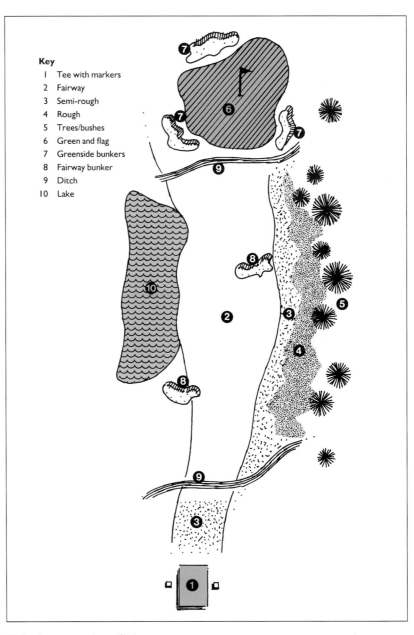

Key

1	Tee with markers
2	Fairway
3	Semi-rough
4	Rough
5	Trees/bushes
6	Green and flag
7	Greenside bunkers
8	Fairway bunker
9	Ditch
10	Lake

Fig 3   A representative golf hole.

strokes. A stroke in golf is the act of striking the ball or even *attempting* to strike it. A miss is termed an 'air shot' and must be counted as a stroke in your score.

Your score is calculated by the number of strokes, or shots, it takes you to get from the teeing area to the green, including sinking your ball in the hole.

Scoring

'Par' is the scoring target for each hole and can be either 3, 4 or 5, depending on the total number of yards between tee and green. A par 3 hole usually has a maximum of 240yd (220m), a par 4 a maximum of 460yd (420m) and a par 5 is any distance above that.

A golf course comprises a combination of par 3s, 4s and 5s to suit the whim of the designer or architect. A course layout could have, for instance, four par 3s, ten par 4s and four par 5s. This would make 72 strokes the *total par* for the course. When you have played all eighteen holes you have played 'a round of golf'.

Some courses can be as short as 5,500yd (5,030m), or less with a par of 60. Other courses can be in excess of 7,000yd (6,400m), veritable 'monsters' for most ordinary golfers, with a par of 73 or 74. The trend these days is to build longer courses so that the word 'Championship' can be applied, thus adding a degree of prestige to the club involved.

COMPETITION

DATE TIME COMP. NO | Handicap | Strokes Rec'd

Player A

Player B

Please indicate which tee used: PAR 70 SSS 70 / PAR 70 SSS 69 / PAR 72 SSS 72

Hole	Marker's Score	White Yards	Par	Yellow Yards	Par	Stroke Index	Ladies Yards	Par	Stroke Index	Score A	Score B	Nett Score A	Nett Score B	W L H-0 POINTS
1		242	3	234	3	7	242	4	17					
2		378	4	370	4	11	355	4	7					
3		437	4	424	4	3	416	4	1					
4		173	3	160	3	15	153	3	11					
5		558	5	551	5	9	475	5	3					
6		473	4	457	4	1	426	5	13					
7		341	4	323	4	13	315	4	9					
8		168	3	150	3	17	127	3	15					
9		387	4	375	4	5	351	4	5					
OUT		3157	34	3044	34		2860	36						
10		296	4	283	4	12	273	4	12					
11		354	4	330	4	10	338	4	10					
12		412	4	397	4	2	358	4	4					
13		296	4	280	4	18	291	4	14					
14		519	5	508	5	6	455	5	8					
15		345	4	327	4	4	308	4	2					
16		326	4	317	4	16	276	4	18					
17		175	3	164	3	8	141	3	16					
18		339	4	331	4	14	336	4	6					
IN		3062	36	2937	36		2776	36						
OUT		3157	34	3044	34		2860	36						
TOT.		6219	70	5981	70		5636	72						

HANDICAP ....

Players Signature .... NETT ....

Markers Signature ....

Copyright Eagle Promotions 01-771 7321

Fig 4 A typical score card.

The Handicap System

Fig 4 shows a typical score card. Most of it will be self-explanatory, except perhaps the column headed by the words 'stroke index', which is simply a means of grading the holes in terms of difficulty. Stroke index is applied when playing against an opponent using the handicap system (at which point you might well ask, 'What is the handicap system?')

Par, however, does not give a fair indication of the difficulty of the course. So a system called 'Standard Scratch Score' (SSS) was instigated to reflect the true value of a player's handicap.

A typical course may have a par of 72, but within that there may be two par 5 holes that, although qualifying in distance as par 5s, are easily reachable in two shots for varying reasons. (For example, they may be downhill, have the prevailing wind behind and not be troubled by out of bounds and awkward bunkers.) These are the 'feel good' holes because even a high handicapper can get the occasional birdie 4. In effect, these holes are really long par 4s.

On the other hand, a par 3 could be 230yd (210m) uphill with the wind against and a huge bunker guarding the green. Most players would have a tough time reaching the green in one stroke, and will feel that it is actually a par 4 hole.

So we now have two par 5 holes that are really par 4s, and one par 3 which is more like a par 4. With these three holes, a simple computation would adjust the par 72 to an SSS of 71. It is against this total, the SSS, that your handicap will be assessed. Put quite simply, a player with a handicap of 10 who scores 81, his 'gross' score, on the above course has produced a 'net' score of 71.

STAR TIP

The main thing is to keep the ball in play – if necessary, play a long par 4 as a par 5.

Ian Woosnam

The maximum handicap is 28 for men and 36 for women. Players competing in a medal round will play 'stroke play' against each other or compete in a field of many players. The winner is the player with the lowest net score; that is, the number of strokes it took to complete the round, minus the handicap.

So golf is a unique game where the *lowest* score wins! In other words, it is the player who makes the fewest mistakes who takes the spoils.

Match Play

Match play is a different format whereby players compete against each other hole by hole, as in the World Match Play Championship, or the biannual Ryder Cup matches between Europe and the USA. The match is determined by the number of holes won rather than total strokes taken. For example, if at the first hole player A scores 4 and his opponent 5, then player A wins the hole and is said to be 'one up'.

Thus the match continues and players who take the same number of strokes at a hole term it a 'half'. The winner is decided when one player is so far ahead that there

> **STAR TIP**
> *In match play, whenever possible, play your approach shot first. In that way you will test your opponent's nerves to better your shot.*
>
> Mark James

are insufficient holes left for his opponent to catch up. However, a match can be 'halved' if both players are even, or 'square', on the number of holes won when the eighteenth hole has been completed. If the match is to be played to a definite conclusion, then both players will play extra holes until someone wins. This is termed a 'sudden death play off', and is also the method for deciding stroke play tournaments.

Handicap golfers refer to the stroke index when they play each other at match play to see when they receive a shot or shots from their opponent. For instance, if a 12 handicap golfer plays a 24 handicapper, the difference in handicaps is obviously twelve strokes. That difference must then be divided by ¾ and it becomes eight (24 − 12 = 12 × ¾ = 8). So the 12 handicapper will have to give his opponent a one-stroke advantage at holes one to eight on the stroke index chart. (There are small variations when players are playing either a 'fourball' or 'foursome' match. This need not bother you at this stage.)

Fourball and Foursome

A fourball is when you choose a partner and team up against two other players. In this case, the best score will count at each hole played. For instance, if you have a 4 and your partner a 3, then his score will count against the best score your opponents can produce.

A foursome is again played with a partner, but in this instance you will play alternate shots using one ball between the two of you. You also take it in turns to drive at alternate holes. For example, you may tee off on the odd holes and your partner on the even. This rotation stays the same no matter who hit the ball last on the previous hole.

Birdies, Eagles and Others

We already know that par is required to score a particular hole. If you improve on that by one stroke you have recorded a 'birdie', which is one under par on a hole.

Two strokes better than par on a hole is called an 'eagle' while three under is termed an 'albatross', a very rare occurrence, even in professional golf. One over par on a hole means you have had a 'bogey'; two over equals a 'double bogey', while more than two strokes is total disaster!

These terms are used very frequently, particularly during television commentaries where professionals often have a 'string of birdies', even an eagle or two.

SCORING CHART			
Par	**Score**		
5	5	=	Par
5	4	=	Birdie
5	3	=	Eagle
5	6	=	Bogey
5	7	=	Double Bogey
5	8	=	Triple Bogey
4	4	=	Par
4	3	=	Birdie
4	2	=	Eagle
4	5	=	Bogey
3	3	=	Par
3	2	=	Birdie
3	1	=	Eagle, or a hole in one!
3	4	=	Bogey

This type of scoring is way beyond the capabilities of the ordinary club golfer, who greets even one birdie as a major event and an eagle as a cause for celebration.

Beginners can expect to bogey their way round with an occasional par when things go right. Make it a practice after the completion of each hole to remind your opponent of the current state of the match by saying, for instance, 'That makes me two up. Correct?' Your opponent might nod, but do not expect a smile!

The phrase 'dormie' is used to indicate that you or your opponent are in a position from which the match cannot be lost. For example, three holes up with only three to play. The golfer in this pleasant position will say something like, 'That makes me dormie three I think'. Do not get complacent. Your opponent could easily rally and halve the match, thus taking you to extra holes. The 19th hole, incidentally, is also a popular term for the clubhouse bar which offers a most welcome sanctuary at the end of a hard round of golf.

CHAPTER 3

EQUIPMENT

Choosing the Right Clubs

As a teacher of golf, I know that a player cannot buy a swing. Once you appreciate that, you will save both time and money, particularly money, when it comes to choosing clubs. Do not be misled into believing that a club that costs £50 is technically better equipped to hit the ball straighter than a club costing £17.50. It is not!

It is difficult to make inaccurate clubs with today's production technology. A club consists of a precision cast head, a shaft and a grip. The manufacturing price at cost at the time of writing is about £2.50. No matter what its selling price.

The difference is so infinitesimal as to make not one iota of difference to anybody, except a low single-figure player or a professional (who will have each club microscopically balanced against the next so that they are 'frequency matched'). They do this because they are precision players. The average player need not be so meticulous.

The vast range of prices that exists for a manufactured club is the result of marketing; nothing else. So when you are starting out do not be hoodwinked by the manufacturers' blurb and do not think that having 'the best money can buy' means you will play better.

Customized Computerized Fitting

This is another attempt to persuade the struggling golfer that a computer can improve his swing by drawing various conclusions from the player's computer readout. It ain't necessarily so!

Computerized fitting fails on two very important fronts:

1. It makes no allowances for the player's stance at the time of fitting, which is crucial to analysing the lie of the club. For instance, a player may have his hands too high or too low because of his incorrect posture. If lessons are taken at a later date, no doubt the faulty address position will be corrected. At a single stroke of good advice, the clubs will all of a sudden become de-customized. The implications are obvious.

2. If you watch a high handicap beginner hammering at the machine you will notice that practically every one of his swings is different. If you add this dimension to the trying out of different so-called models and swing weights, then by the time the player has finished, the result in the majority of cases is a purely romantic conclusion.

The answer to 'customizing' is to see your local professional. A club professional has the ability to measure you and your swing without resorting to computer technology and, if necessary, correct your address position so that the lie can be assessed from a proper standpoint.

Swing Weights and Shaft Flex

Provided that you are not in the extremes of age or brutally strong, there is not too much to be done about swing weights or shaft flex.

There is no need either to be concerned with comparison of shaft performance. For instance, you will see tests showing the 'scatter capabilities' of shafts when balls are hit by the Iron Byron swing machines. It is fine relating these figures to a touring pro, but totally inappropriate for them to be applied to the weekend golfer whose scatter

capabilities are an inescapable way of golfing life. Therefore, it is a totally meaningless comparison.

It is advisable, however, to be checked if you are tall or short, but let this be done, again, by your local friendly professional – not a machine.

Study the illustration of the correct lie as shown opposite. Notice how the toe of the club is off the ground. This is important because when the club returns to the impact position, the shaft bends downwards, thus flattening out the blade angle. Many players make the understandable mistake at address of ensuring that the bottom of the club is flat on the ground. This will make the toe of the club stick in the ground at impact, spinning it open and causing a slice.

Keeping the clubhead flat on the ground at address will also encourage the player to hold the hands too high, stiffening the hand and arm action – a typical address fault.

KIT CHECK

If you are a beginner taking the game seriously and of average height and build, by all means buy off the shelf. There is also absolutely no need to buy a full set, that is, nine irons. Save money by buying a half set. This means choosing either the (3), 5, 7, 9 wedge, or 4, 6, 8 wedge. The wedge can either be sand or pitching. (I have bracketed the no. 3 iron because this is not essential until your swing has settled in to a reasonable line to the ball.)

Four irons instead of a full set of nine are enough to start with. Why not buy the lot? Buying a full set is not necessary because a beginner or struggling handicap player can never guarantee what distance he is going

Fig 5   This is how the shaft bends at impact.

to hit the ball: it can vary by as much as 30yd (27m) per club.

Once you improve your technique, you will have a better idea of how far you hit with each club. Then you will have earned the right to indulge yourself.

Of course, if you are offered a reasonable set of second-hand irons at a fair price, then snap them up. They could be used later in a part-exchange deal.

KIT CHECK
The best design for beginners is certainly the 'Game Improver' model. This incorporates features that help the beginner. The following examples are just some of the features these clubs offer and that you should look out for:

1.   Peripheral, cavity back which spreads the sweet spot (that part of the clubface which makes contact with the ball) so that off-line hits do not sting your fingers.
2.   The main weight mass is at base of head to help get the ball airborne quicker.
3.   A raised trailing edge and white-lined leading edge to help alignment.
4.   An overall bigger hitting surface to promote confidence and allow more margin for error.

All these features do not guarantee that you will hit the ball straight, no matter what the hand-outs say!

If you suspect that you are not standard size, your best bet is to seek professional advice and be fitted with a few irons to suit your build. Many pros offer this service at no extra charge, particularly on beginners' clubs. This allows the starter to build the set up month by month from the same model.

Choosing a Wood

This can be either of the metal or laminate variety. A laminate wood will be quite adequate and is about half the price of a metal wood. (Yes, metal wood. Nobody has yet thought up another name.)

A set of woods these days consists of numbers 1, 3, and 5. The numbers 2 and 4

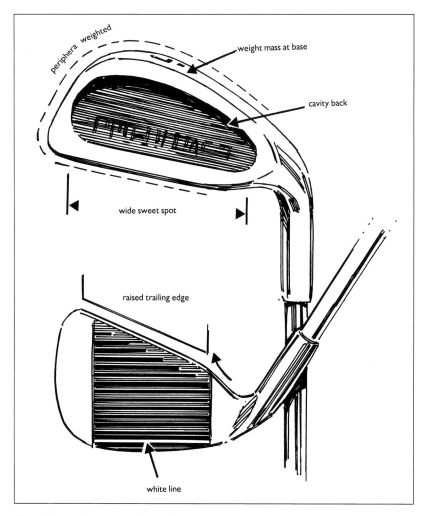

Fig 6   Cavity back irons – best for the beginner.

are virtually extinct because the modern range can be supplied in various 'in-between' lofts. You will also come across a no. 7 wood, which is equal to a no. 5 iron for distance but flights the ball higher. Likewise the no. 5 wood is a useful substitute for the no. 3 iron.

As a beginner, do not be tempted to buy a driver in expectation of greater distance: it will not happen. A no. 3 wood is an ideal substitute during your early development. Only when you have the technique to bring the clubhead squarely to the back of the ball with your body behind it will you be competent enough to

use a driver. So do not kid yourself. Most handicappers would knock ten shots off their score if they left the no. 1 wood at home!

For example, Nick Faldo frequently plays an entire round using his driver only once or twice. He cannot always rely on hitting the ball accurately enough with it. If *he* can admit to that fact, so can you!

This does not mean you should never buy a driver. It means, *be patient*. You will know when it is the right time: namely, when you have the confidence to use one.

Your first driver should have a minimum of 12 degrees loft. Do not be tempted by

'tour loft' and 'tour grind', or any other such descriptions of de-lofted drivers. As the names imply, they are designed to be used exclusively by touring professionals!

Putters

Here you are quite at liberty to indulge yourself from the wondrous selection of different sizes and shapes of heads. Not to mention the broom-handle-length models!

As a starter it would perhaps be preferable to select one from the three basic models: ping shape, centre shaft or blade. Even here there is a certain amount of interbreeding. The answer is to try them out in the pro shop or adjacent putting green, if allowed, before deciding on your purchase.

> **KEY POINT**
> The best guide of all when it comes to putting is . . . If it feels right, it is right!

Whilst you may gain an affection for the first putter you buy, I guarantee that before the end of your career you will have a cupboard or attic full of rejects. Never do affairs so quickly fade as when your favourite putter lets you down, so pick a cheap one if you have a short fuse!

Golf Bags

If you want to indulge yourself when you can play, fine, but as an apprentice to the game you really do not need a huge bag. You will recall I recommended you to start with a half set of of clubs, say five irons, a wood and a putter. Not only would they be lost in a big bag, but there is the cost to consider.

If you choose a pro-style bag you will then need a trolley, or extremely strong shoulders and legs to carry it round nearly three miles. The sensible alternative is to select a good quality collapsible bag or a nylon lightweight model. Both these styles are easily carried on the shoulder and add very little extra weight to your long walk.

The further advantage of a carry-bag is

that you can go anywhere on the course. A bag on a trolley means many detours. For instance, you will have to walk around every green and tee, you will not be able to take your bag in the rough and you will have to look for a bridge when you come to a ditch rather than just step over.

As a beginner, you do not need this extra aggravation! It also adds to today's slow play problems. One of the most harrowing and frustrating sights on the golf course is that of looking down the fairway and seeing four huge pro bags on trolleys parked at various quarters of the fairway, but not a golfer in sight. They are all out there in the jungle searching for their mishits!

You may be surprised to learn that many assistant pros prefer to carry their clubs in lightweight bags when playing a casual round.

Golf Shoes

The best advice is *get them*! You cannot play golf without a pair. Many professionals will not even give you a lesson unless you are wearing a pair of spiked golf shoes. I agree. Good footwear is vital because a good swing starts from the feet up. The cheapest shoes are injection moulded plastic. They are totally waterproof but are inclined to be heavy. Many claim they hurt your feet. This could be true on a hot day, but they can be very comfortable if you are forced to play in inclement weather with lashing rain and a howling wind. Cheap, hot and heavy they may be, but far better than the universal trainers, which

> **KIT CHECK**
> Although you may pay half as much again, the better shoes are worth it in the long run. The uppers are normally-treated leather, while the soles are man-made plastic. Better still, they come in a variety of attractive designs and colour. In addition, the leather is treated with water-repellant so your feet will stay dry except in the most adverse conditions. Golf shoes can now be as comfortable as your trainers; they can also be obtained in genuine fully-cushioned trainer style.

the serious golfer should never contemplate wearing.

I recommend that you use a spiked rather than pimple soled shoe for two reasons:

1. Spikes allow you a firm, safe footing no matter what the conditions or the severity of the slope.
2. Spikes are better for greens than pimple soles, particularly if the surface is soft. In fact, some courses ban the pimples.

Balls

My advice to beginners is to take your pick from the 'pick-ups'. Do not waste your time trying to convince yourself that you need what the manufacturers say you need. At beginner or high handicap level it makes not the slightest difference what you use, provided it is 1.68in (4cm) in diameter and dimpled.

If you want to delve into the performances of various dimple patterns from a scientific viewpoint, fine, but a mishit ball still goes crooked. As 99 per cent of shots enter that category, what does it matter which ball you play? But if you have to choose, seek a two-piece Surlyn-covered ball from the medium price bracket.

Do not waste your money on the Balata three-piece balls that tournament pros play. The outer layer is very soft and a slight mishit could render the ball unplayable. The ball is also designed to take spin, and that can work against you as it will accentuate the flight on any misdirected shot. Finally, the Balata ball does not go as far as the Surlyn two-piece and beginners never want to lose distance!

> **KIT CHECK**
> While you are learning, your best bet is to select from the tub of USA pond balls on show in most pro shops. They have usually only been hit once before being lost, found and re-marketed. They are great value for money.

Equipment Summary

1. Clubs: a reasonably-priced half set, checked by your local pro.
2. Bag: why not carry? It is easy on the legs and softer on the pocket.
3. Balls: there is much talk on the subject – pick a pond ball until you can really play.

CHAPTER 4

RULES AND PROCEDURES

Before you venture on to the course, you must know the laws or Rules of Golf, which are determined by the Royal and Ancient Golf Club at St Andrews, Scotland, in conjunction with the United States Golf Association. You must obtain this valuable booklet, read it thoroughly and carry it in your golf bag at all times.

Essential Rules

It is beyond the scope of this book to detail all the rules of golf, but it is important that you are made aware of some of the bare essentials.

The rules of golf also contain an important section on etiquette, or good manners. Every golfer should familiarize himself with this small section of the rule book. They are not rules *per se*, but guidelines as to the proper procedure on the course. One of the reasons why golf has so far avoided the deterioration of conduct and bad sportsmanship displayed in other major spectator sports and events is due largely to golfers heeding the section on etiquette.

Professional golfers are renowned for their honesty and integrity in calling a foul upon themselves. Indeed, many breaches of the rules go unseen. If, for example, the ball moves once the player has taken his address position, it counts as an extra shot. It may seem unjust and nobody may have seen the ball move, but this particular rule is there to prevent unscrupulous golfers 'accidentally on purpose' improving their lie; that is, moving the ball to a slightly better spot.

Many of the rules are made to encourage players to take the good breaks with the bad with equanimity.

Let us play a few imaginary holes of golf played in the company of an experienced partner, looking at the proper procedures and also some of the problems that often arise in actual play.

Observe Etiquette

You join the queue on the first tee with your new set of clubs and see someone you know. You go to speak but are nudged in the ribs because there is a golfer about to play from the tee. One important rule to observe is that of silence when another golfer is about to play. That means that you must not even fiddle with your golf bag, as an accidental 'clank' may disturb the player's concentration. This is good manners and consideration for other players.

RULES CHECK
You must remain silent while a golfer plays his shots.

The Honour

Eventually it is your turn to approach the tee and your partner has decided to give you the privilege, or 'honour', of playing first. Who plays first is usually decided by the toss of a coin. In some cases, however, the player with the lowest handicap will take the honour. You take your trolley onto the teeing area only to discover that this is forbidden. Never take a trolley onto the teeing ground.

Where to Tee Up

Humbly, you wheel it back, select your club and return to the tee, making sure to tee up in line with, or behind, the two tee box markers which define the area in which you can legally play the ball from. You may tee the ball anywhere up to two club lengths behind the two markers and your feet may be positioned outside this area but never the ball.

Once you have balanced the ball on the peg, your practice swing accidentally takes a lump out of the hallowed teeing ground. Only then does someone draw your attention to a small notice board which states 'No practice swinging on the tee'.

'Accidents' on the Tee

If you now knock the ball off the tee when you put the clubhead behind the ball, an onlooker will inevitably call out 'One!' (the standard response in this situation). There is no penalty for moving the ball during your pre-swing routine *on the tee*. You can tee it up again. Haste makes you take a quick swipe and you miss the ball. Remember, an air shot counts as a stroke, so that you have played one stroke even though your ball is still on the tee.

Out of Bounds

You then send the ball veering out of bounds on your next shot, which is when you learn about stroke and distance, meaning that you have to hit another ball. This next stroke must be played after your partner has hit his shot. You watch as he plays, and then play again. Much to your delight the ball flies down the fairway, but you have taken four strokes to get there: one air shot, one out of bounds, a penalty for doing so, and one to put the ball in the fairway.

STAR TIP
Concentrate fully on the shot you are about to play and forget what has gone before.
Ian Woosnam

Who Plays Next?

When you locate your ball it is 30yd behind your partner's. You must play first when this happens as the rules dictate that the player farthest from the flag plays first.

You notice that your ball is nestling against a twig and, innocently and without thinking, bend down and remove it. Your ball rolls backward just a fraction and you find out that this too costs you a stroke. Had it simply turned on its own axis, you would have been alright. Dejected, you mishit your next shot 20yd along the ground and it is still your turn to play because you have not reached your partner's ball.

> **RULES CHECK**
> The ball furthest from the flag is always played first.

Procedure in the Sand

This time, you connect with a reasonably good iron shot towards the green, only to see it fall into a bunker.

When you arrive at the sand trap, you find to your dismay that your ball is lying in a footmark. 'Bad luck,' says your partner, 'The previous player should have used the rake provided or at least have smoothed the sand out with his foot or club after he had played.'

You climb into the trap, remembering to wiggle your feet into the sand and open your stance. You even remember not to ground the club because you know the rules forbid you to touch the sand with a club.

You are not positive enough when playing out of the sand and accidentally hit the ball while it is in the air, leaving the ball in the trap. 'That's another shot', your partner replies. 'Even though you didn't mean it, you hit it twice and they all count.'

Casual Water

Your next effort gets the ball onto the green where it lands in a puddle of water. 'More bad luck', you moan, but this time

you are lucky. Puddles are termed 'casual water' under the rules and you can move your ball to the nearest point of relief, making sure it is no nearer the hole.

The Flagstick

You are now requested to hold the flag while your partner takes his first putt. You try to remove the flag as the ball approaches the hole, but the pole will not budge and is struck by the ball. In this instance, you have cost your partner a stroke, who tells you that the rules state that the ball must not strike the flagstick while putting.

Although you tended the flag, removing the flagstick is the player's responsibility. However, no penalty is incurred if the flagstick is struck when playing a shot from off the green.

> **RULES CHECK**
> The green is the only place where you are allowed to mark and clean the ball.

Repairing the Green

You are now dejected and embarrassed but you decide to try to sink your putt. You replace the ball carefully but notice a few spike marks on your line to the hole. Before your partner can stop you, you have tapped them down with the head of the putter only to hear 'Sorry, but that has cost you another stroke.'

> **RULES CHECK**
> You can repair pitch marks, but not spike marks.

Play Without Delay

Now red-faced and inwardly fuming, you once again get ready to putt. Your partner holds the stick, placing one hand at the top of the pole to stop the flag from fluttering in the wind. With the other he gently loosens the stick so that it will easily come out. To better see the line of

> **RULES CHECK**
> Golfers must play without undue delay.

the putt, you lower yourself onto your haunches, just as you have seen the professionals do it on TV. You are just about to plumb the line with your putter shaft when your partner again brings you back down to earth. 'I am sorry to mention it, but we are holding up play. Just putt out quickly. I mean, it isn't really worth bothering about when you are putting for an eleven!'

Always Know the Rules

You make the putt and then discover that you have left your trolley in front of the green, another mistake. You try to make up for lost time by running back to collect it and notice some golfers watching you with hands on hips and shaking their heads.

'Did I really take eleven?', you ask your partner. 'Yes, but three of those strokes were because you didn't know the rules.'

In fact, a lot of golfers, experienced golfers even, break the rules most of the time. Many of the scores they return will be pure fiction. For instance, when a player has a legitimate right to pick up the ball and drop it, some will just toss it down or even kick it into place. The correct procedure is to hold the ball out at shoulder height in line with the hole and then to drop it.

Many players break the rules because they want to speed up play. This, too, is against the rules. *Players may not agree among themselves to waive the rules of golf.* In other words; you either have to play the game properly or not at all.

As this one imaginary hole indicates, knowing the rules can save you not only strokes, but also a great deal of embarrassment. So, get a copy of the rules as soon as you can!

It is also a good idea, especially as a beginner, to try to play with experienced, low-handicap golfers and learn to stick to the rules until rules and procedures become second nature. Under no circumstances should you tolerate taking liberties with the laws of golf.

PART 2
THE LONG GAME

CHAPTER 5

FAULTS AND CURES

It is foolhardy to offer a cure for a particular ailment without seeing a golfer swing. Take the classic slice, for instance. All untrained beginners slice the ball; that is, they send it veering off to the right. The standard cures offer to either turn the hands to the right, or hit from 'inside to out'. What is totally ignored in this advice is the fundamental flaw that haunts all high handicap golfers: namely, that they have not yet learned to control the shoulders or the over-reaction of the right side of the body. Neither are the hands educated to control and use the club throughout the swing action. In other words, what a player requires first and foremost is proper and thorough training.

It is not the purpose of this book to list the so-called cures to faults such as 'coming over the top' and 'hitting early' among others. It is hoped that by sticking to concise instructions we will stop faults happening in the first place. However, there is a 'trouble shooting' section (*see* Chapter 14) to help you identify typical beginners' problems. When coaching pupils, I will invariably return to my special set of basic fundamentals with the result that swing faults simply melt away. In that way, too, I eventually get to the very core of the problem, which can then be removed forever.

Ball Direction and Flight

The straight or drawn shots are regarded as the most desirable, although some touring pros cultivate a controlled 'fade'. Here is a variety of shots to whet your imagination.

This chart has been included for purely educational purposes. It is beyond the scope of this book to explain exactly what

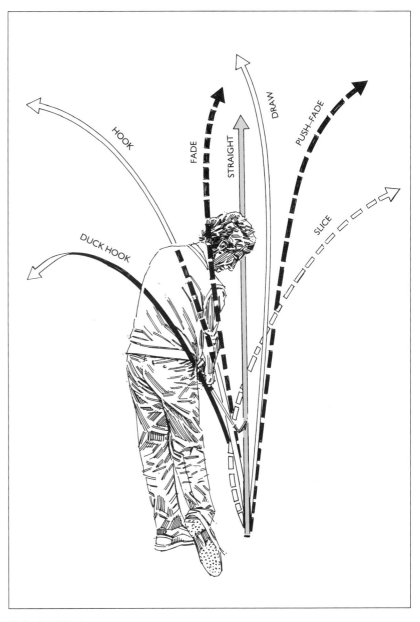

Fig 7   Ball flight chart.

causes the ball to go off at unintended tangents because treating such shots symptomatically is no cure for an ailing swing.

Many 'quick-cure charts' have been drawn up with advice such as: 'If your ball is slicing, then strengthen your grip and/or hit more from the inside.' I personally regard this sort of advice as totally spurious because it does not take into account the root-cause of the fault which is nine times out of ten a bad address position and/or a misshapen swing. 'Meddling' from that standpoint is asking for trouble. It can only make matters worse – and frequently does.

However, study the chart on Fig 7, remembering that your goal is to learn to produce that straight shot, but do not worry if, during your training period, you go through the whole spectrum; that, as any experienced golfer will tell you, is par for the course!

Swing Shape

What do I mean by 'swing shape'? Swing shape is simply a more precise way of describing the overall look of a swing, as seen by a trained or experienced eye.

When watching tournament pros practising before an event, I often point out to pupils a swing that shows class and consistency. Likewise, I identify the swings which have a bad shape and no hope of competing at the highest level.

Nick Faldo is one world class player who changed his 'shape'. He had what is known in the trade as a dipped left shoulder and a crossed line at the top. However, he worked at improving his shoulder angle and putting his club on line at the top, therefore changing the shape of his swing to one that would work more consistently. Nick's new shape is an excellent one to copy.

You only have to observe what you see around you to notice the difference between a good swing shape and a bad one. Apply yourself to copy the best. Do

Fig 8 (a)   Nick Faldo demonstrates his old swing shape, showing his club 'crossed line' at the top . . .

Fig 8 (b)   . . . and his new backswing shape – a good model to copy.

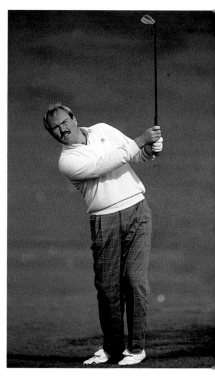

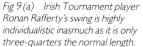

Fig 9 (a)   Irish Tournament player Ronan Rafferty's swing is highly individualistic inasmuch as it is only three-quarters the normal length.

Fig 9 (b)   But he makes up for it with supreme hand action and timing.

Fig 9 (c)   Rafferty's unique style is not recommended to the beginner who wishes to learn a more standardized swing.

not hesitate to ask advice from a qualified teacher – but never follow amateurs. Seeing yourself on video can also be an eye-opener and is well worth investigating.

The Shape of Swings to Come

Most professionals look reasonably similar to the untrained eye, with the exception of some very individualistic swings such as

> **KEY POINT**
> A bad swing cannot be corrected at the stroke of a pen! Swing faults can only be cured through regular sessions with an experienced tutor. In this way, the correct technique can be acquired by means of intense instruction and, above all, physical demonstration.

those belonging to Lee Trevino, Arnold Palmer, Sandy Lyle and Mark James.

However, even the above-mentioned players share a good basic shape in the crucial parts of their swing.

My job is to inform you on which parts to copy, which to ignore, and why. You will then arrive at a basic composite swing shape devoid of all unnecessary and gratuitous embellishments.

Once the shape is fixed in your mind, you will have to work at exercises which will enable you to develop the basic shape and make it work for you.

CHAPTER 6

AN INTRODUCTION TO THE ADDRESS POSITION

The swing shape starts at the address position. Reading this section is the first test of your resolution to learn the golf swing properly and thoroughly, because you will be tempted to skim through this part and get into the interesting bit of hitting the ball. *Resist this temptation*! It is absolutely vital that you stand correctly to the ball and, more importantly, understand why this is so necessary.

Ninety-nine per cent of all golfers who present themselves to me for lessons have a bad address position – that includes posture, arm set and grip. The truth of the matter is that the majority will make an immediate improvement by simply correcting this aspect of their swing. Another simple fact is that many established players constantly search through reams of instruction books and videos looking for the elusive answers to their swing problems. The last thing they consider is their address position, particularly their posture. Unless this part is attended to as a priority, there is no point in tampering with any other section of the swing.

So, condition your mind now to read, re-read and study this chapter with all the concentration at your disposal.

Before taking a club in your hand you must spend a little time concentrating on your body posture. I stress this as an indispensable prelude to your education as a golfer with a future. Although you may be eager to get a club in your hands right away, try to be patient and concentrate on the exercises that follow.

Fig 10   Make this the model for your set-up and grip.

STAR TIP
Always use a strict pre-shot routine.
                                        Ian Woosnam

Practice Exercise

Stand erect with your legs apart the width of your shoulders. At this early stage, there must not be the slightest hint of a slouch, or a stomach out. So keep your chest up and shoulders back, your stomach muscles pulled in and your back and legs straight.

Lean forward as if to bow in oriental fashion, but do not drop your chest. Now push your posterior back. Your posterior must go back as a counter balance.

Flex the knees slightly. Ensure that the head has not dropped.

Let your arms hang freely with the upper arms away from your body. At first, this position will feel strange, but you must practise it frequently until it becomes natural. (This final position is in no way to be compared with the misleading 'sitting on bar stool' adage which causes many golfers to take liberties with their address positions.)

> **KIT CHECK**
> Always make sure that your golf clubs suit your stature.

Apart from the initial discomfort, your attitude should be one of physical alertness, similar to that of a soccer player poised to face an oncoming opponent, a cricketer in the slips or a tennis player about to receive a serve. The feeling of alertness is vital to awakening and stimulating your mind and body to the task in hand.

Above all, ignore advice that says 'Take a comfortable position', as this will surely hamper your progress.

Fig 11 (a)   Stand erect, legs apart the width of your shoulders.
Fig 11 (b)   Lean forward, chest up, bottom back!
Fig 11 (c)   Flex knees slightly.
Fig 11 (d)   Let arms hang freely from your body.
Fig 11 (e)   Don't adopt a 'bar stool' position. Compare this with the correct posture shown in Figs 11 (c) and (d).

Figs 11 (a)–(e)   The address position.

(a)

(b)

(c)

(d)

(e)

Fig 12 (a)   A good address position.

Fig 12 (b)   A typically bad address position.

Good and Bad Posture

Study the photographs on this page of a young pupil in a good address position and compare it with the author adopting a typically bad one! You will get a better idea of what constitutes good and bad posture.

> **KEY POINT**
> Adopt a perfect address position. Nothing less will do.

Copy professionals such as Lee Trevino, Hale Irwin, Tom Weiskopf, Tom Watson, Jack Nicklaus, Seve Ballesteros and Nick Faldo, all major championship winners.
Practising in front of a mirror is a good aid to developing sound posture, because what a posture feels like is not necessarily what it looks like! Pupils are constantly surprised and delighted by seeing their corrected address position in a mirror.

> **KIT CHECK**
> A mirror is an invaluable teaching aid to which you should constantly refer.

You may be slightly embarrassed by sticking your bottom out, but it looks totally right and professional when viewed in the mirror with the completed address position.

Fig 13   Seve Ballesteros – an address position to copy.

Free the Arms to Swing

KEY POINT
Your arms should be hanging freely in front of you. They should also be slightly bowed outwards, not inwards.

Now that we have dealt with posture, let us concentrate on your arms. If you have adopted the correct posture as outlined on page 26, you will have your chest up, your stomach muscles in, your bottom back and your knees slightly flexed.

Let your arms hang freely in front of you, with the elbows slightly bowed outwards. Get used to this feeling of freedom. At no time must you be tempted to follow the trend of some golfers to twist or contort your arms inwards, or to connect the upper arms to your body. As a beginner, this will severely hamper your progress. (I shall deal with the reasons for this in greater detail later.)

For the moment, accept that your arms must be given the capacity to swing. To help you to achieve this feeling, practise the following exercises regularly.

Fig 14 Arms bowed out and clear of the chest.

UP – DOWN – SLOWLY

Fig 15 A vital freeing exercise.

Practice Exercise
Start in the correct address position. Now swing your arms up to shoulder height and down again to your waist. Do this slowly as if you are levering your arms up and down.

Ensure that you do not lift your body during this exercise by keeping your head still and height constant throughout.

At first, you may feel a slight discomfort in your lower back; this is not harmful: you are merely activating some new golf muscles. (The back is a source of power.) You may also feel pressure at the back of your legs. This, too, is natural because you are gaining experience of resistance in the lower half of your body.

What you are in effect doing is learning to swing your arms *independently* from your body. This is not easy and must be learned.

Later on you will be doing this exercise

with a club in your hands and will learn to refer to this most crucial of all exercises many times.

You perhaps do not have a vast amount of spare time nor a practice range at your disposal, but you can cut corners by working at freeing your arms with this simple exercise. The benefits will become apparent as you go through your lessons, particularly when you apply this concept to the start of the downswing. This will put you way ahead of the pack!

Grip and Arm-Set

I have listed the arm-set and grip together quite deliberately because they are closely linked. By 'arm-set', I mean the precise position of your arms in relation to your body and your target line.

Let us deal with the grip first. Basically, there are three different types of grip:

1. The Vardon or overlapping.
2. The ten-finger or baseball.
3. The interlocking grip.

By far the most popular is the overlapping or Vardon grip. A small proportion of players use the interlocking grip. Jack Nicklaus is the most famous interlocker of all; he finds it easier to use that grip because he has small hands. However, many players who also have small hands use the overlapping grip without encountering too many problems.

In general, the average player would be advised to avoid the interlocking grip

Fig 16 (a)   The Vardon or overlapping grip – the most popular grip of all.

Fig 16 (b)   The Vardon grip from a different angle.

Fig 17 The interlocking grip – the grip used by Jack Nicklaus.

Fig 18 Do not interlock too deeply. Notice that the fingers have lost alignment, causing a 'ham-handed' grip.

because it can lead to interlocking too deeply. The player ends up with a ham-handed or palm grip, thus losing all sensitivity in his fingers.

The ten-finger grip tends to encourage the hands to work independently, which is the opposite of what we want.

So, let us not make it difficult for ourselves and let us stick to the overlapping grip.

The most functional and efficient way for your hands to work is when they are

---

KEY POINT

The hands work best palm to palm.

---

linked together palm to palm, with the back of the left hand facing the target and the right palm matching it.

All you need to do now is to move your right hand below your left and you have the makings of the perfect grip with the palms parallel to each other at all times.

Let us deal with the grip in more detail.

Fig 19 (a) The ten-finger or baseball grip. This grip tends to make the hands work against each other.

Fig 19 (b) A different view of the ten-finger grip.

Fig 20 Keep the hands working palm to palm, the back of the left hand facing the target.

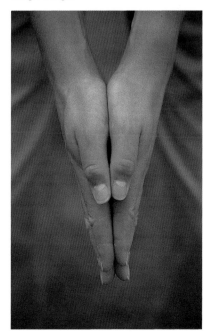

Figs 21 (a)–(h)   Left-side control.

The Left Hand and Forearm

Set the club, say a no. 5 iron, on the ground and support it with the right forefinger and thumb.

Keep the leading edge at right angles to your intended line, making sure that the face of the club points directly at the target.

Try not to get confused by the trailing edge, which is optically confusing and tempts many golfers to incorrectly align the club pointing to the left of target. Your grip must always be related to the face of the club.

Place your left hand and fingers on the grip, arranging your hand at an angle of about 45 degrees.

Balance the club across the middle pad of your index finger and heel pad (not thumb pad).

Now gently wrap your hand over the grip, positioning the thumb initially on the top of the grip and leaving about half an inch spare at the top end.

Now turn your left hand very slightly to the right without disturbing the clubhead. This will have the important effect of firming up the muscles of the forearm and hand so that they will work as one controllable unit and develop the power to sustain firm action through impact. (You will note that the arm is slightly bowed, the muscles activated. When viewed from the front or in a mirror, you will see two and a half knuckles on your left hand.)

Now lift the club from the ground and hold it in front of you, noting the slight angle between the arms and shaft. This is never a straight line, a common misconception in untrained golfers.

Lift your thumb and feel the genuine support given by the heel pad and the pressure of the last three fingers. Lower the thumb once more.

Fig 21 (a)   Left-hand grip from behind. Lift the club from the ground to check firmness of grip.

Fig 21 (b)   The face of the club must point at the target.

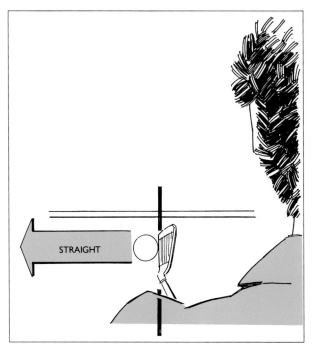

Fig 21 (c)   A common error – the face of the club points left.

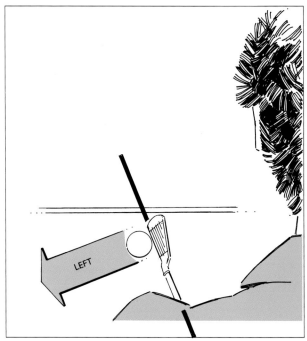

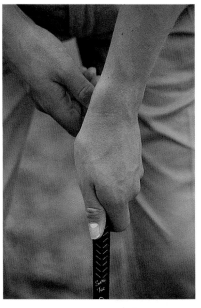

Fig 21 (d)   Your left hand should be at an angle of 45 degrees. Balance the club across the index finger and heel pad.

Fig 21 (e)   Position the thumb initially on the top of the grip.

Fig 21 (f)   Turn the hand to the right to complete the left hand grip. Two and a half knuckles should be seen from the front.

Fig 21 (g)   The heel pad pressure test.

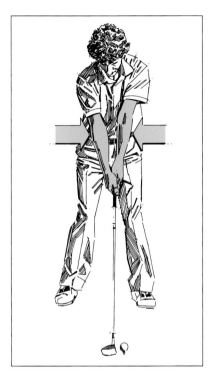

Fig 22   Never twist the elbows inwards. Doing so will hinder your swing.

You should now practise moving your arm up and down. This will give an initial insight into the role of the left arm and left side control, which will be explained later in the downswing exercises.

Such control is not achieved by making the left arm stiff and rigid. Comfortable leverage with your left arm is not possible if your left arm is made too tense, or, worse, twisted inwards because the elbow joint is then in its weakest position.

Much of golfers' 'tennis elbow' can be traced to an unnatural arm-lock position. Yet I have actually seen keen golf students being recommended to forcefully twist both elbows inwards and then expected to swing a club freely! One person described it as a particularly painful variation of a wrestler's arm-lock hold. This is an example of what *not* to copy! I hope this in itself will deter you from venturing down that most dangerous road.

The Right Hand

It is now time to position your right hand and arm. I would like you to imagine that you are going to use a racquet; after all, golf is really a bat and ball game. Take note of how the right palm faces directly at the intended target. Notice too how the right elbow is positioned downwards. Using the same theory, but this time imagining that the palm of your hand is the face of a racquet, note again how the right shoulder has lowered naturally.

It is important that you do not try to keep the shoulders level, as this will inhibit your backswing.

Form your right hand grip by first linking the middle two fingers round the grip, letting the little finger overlap the crevice between the index and third finger of your left hand.

Allow your thumb pad to sit gently on the thumb of your left hand. Finally, arrange your right index finger and thumb to join the grip as shown in Fig 23 (d). Notice that the thumb sits on the left-hand or target side of the grip, and the tip of your index finger forms a crook, and touches or almost touches the ball of your thumb.

Avoid extending your index finger downwards, or treating it as a trigger finger. Such a position leads to many technical problems. Remember that we are trying to eliminate all exaggerations from the swing you are going to learn, so keep that finger in the right place!

This also applies to the position of the right thumb. *Never* place it on the top of the handle of the club. Proper wrist break is impossible with the right thumb down the grip; it also hinders the proper use of the hands. To confirm this, you will not find an Open Champion past or present sporting his right thumb on top. Jack Nicklaus, undoubtedly one of the greatest golfers of modern times, practically dismisses his thumb, getting it well out of the way. This is particularly noticeable at both the top of his swing and at impact. The job of the finger and thumb is to help support the club at the top of the backswing, nothing else.

You should now have your hands correctly positioned on the club.

Figs 23 (a)–(f) Positioning the right hand and arm.

Fig 23 (a)   The right palm faces directly at the target.

Fig 23 (d)   The completed overlapping grip.

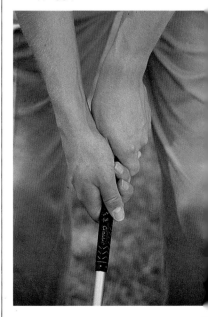

Fig 23 (b)   The right hand should be applied as if using a racquet.

Fig 23 (e)   Avoid the 'trigger' finger.

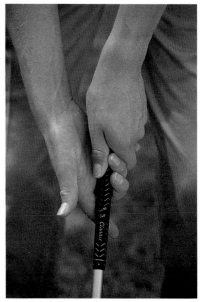

Fig 23 (c)   Link the middle two fingers and let the little finger overlap.

Fig 23 (f)   Never place the right thumb in this position: it hinders proper use of the hands.

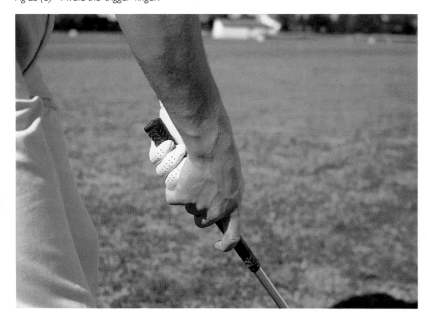

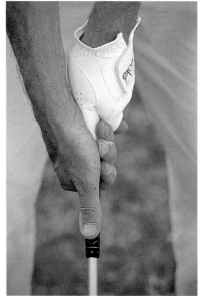

Grip Pressure

It is very difficult to convey in words just
how light the grip pressure should be, but
holding lightly can be compared to the
strength required to hold a fledgeling in
your hands without harming it.

If a top professional were to offer his
club to you, you could pull it easily from his
grasp. Try the same with the average
amateur and it would become a tug of
war! This is because *amateurs* believe they
must hold it tight to control it.

Gripping the club too tightly has the
very opposite effect. Excessive pressure
not only renders the fingers totally
insensitive, but also creates initial tension
which then spreads like a steel girdle
throughout the rest of the body. Such
tension can cause a multitude of wayward
shots. But do not get alarmed if you feel
the need to grip tightly. It is only natural
that you would want to do so.

*Fig 24   In a good grip, the club should
run along the parallel groove of both hands.*

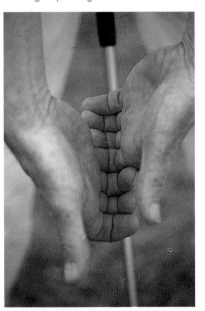

You must get to work to undo this
tendency immediately by working at
strengthening your hands via the exercises
in Chapter 19. When your hands are
stronger you will feel confident enough
not to hold the club in a vice-like grip.

A top player at all times senses the
position of the club throughout the swing.
He seemingly performs the miracle of
effortless control that baffles the high
handicap player. This is possible because
he holds the club with a sensitive grip.

Study this photo sequence for a double
demo exercise. Notice how, when I open
my hands, the club could run along the
groove created by the fingers. Note how
the grooves are misaligned in a faulty grip.

Another adaptation of this exercise is
for you to open and shut your hands by
gently folding them to form your grip. In
this way, the hands and wrists will work
fluently and will gain maximum power
through the ball.

Pressure Points

The pressure points in the grip are the last
three fingers of the left hand and the
middle two fingers of the right hand.
There should be no pressure with the

*Fig 25   The misaligned fingers of a
bad grip.*

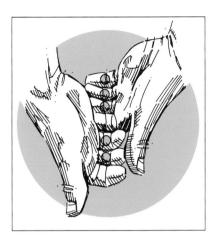

*Fig 26   These are the pressure points
when holding the club.*

finger and thumb of the right hand. The
above rule is not disputed by the vast
majority of world class players and
teachers.

Please do not be deceived by recent
(1990) regression to the right index finger
as a trigger. This was a 1920s and 1930s
gimmick and still rears its ugly digit from
time to time. It is positively harmful and
leads many golfers to release the clubhead
too early in the swing sequence.

Now revise this chapter and remind
yourself of the main points:

1. Your posture at address is chest up,
bottom back, stomach in, knees flexed and
your head in a natural position, not down.
Your body should be alert and your arms
free to swing.
2. The left forearm muscles are firmed up
and both arms are bowed out slightly. The
right arm stays passive, the elbow turned
down with the palm to the target. There
should be absolutely no stiffness.
3. The palms are together and square to
the target line. You will be holding on to
the club gently, with no trigger finger and
no thumb on top.

CHAPTER 7

ALIGNMENT AND BALL POSITION

We have gone through the crucial elements of the address position including posture, arm-set and grip. Now we must make sure to point the club in the right direction. This means getting your alignment correct. One of the simplest ways of doing this is to practise the following exercise.

Practice Exercise
Place two golf clubs on the ground parallel to each other and pointing down the target line. Grip the club and ensure that your arm-set is correct.

Fig 27 (a)   Preparation for the correct address position. (b) As you bend forward, push the bottom back and keep the chest up. (c) Lower the club to the ground without altering your arm-set or grip. You now have the perfect address position.

Now line your toes up against one of the clubs and arrange your body so that your feet, hips and shoulders are also parallel. Do this with the club already in your hands so that you may now extend your arms in front of you, making sure that there is an angle between your arms and the shaft and that the leading edge of the clubhead is vertical. This will ensure that the clubface is at right angles to the line of flight when it is grounded. Get used to viewing the blade in this way; it is an invaluable guide to keeping the clubface square at address.

Your next step is to bend forward from the waist, with the legs straight and maintaining the arm-set and correct posture. Do not hunch the shoulders or drop your head. Keep your bottom

pushed back and then flex the knees without crouching or sitting down.

Finally, lower the clubhead to the ground without altering your arm-set or grip.

This set-up procedure will also ensure that you stand the correct distance from the ball. Check your final address in a mirror.

The natural position of the ball for all irons from the sand wedge to the no. 5 iron is mid-way between the feet. Above that, the ball should be positioned progressively forward in the stance for long irons and woods, until the ball is opposite the left heel for the driver.

Never play or practise hitting the ball further back than the centre of the stance unless you are playing special shots.

(b)

(c)

ball placement

short irons

fairway woods and
long irons

driver

Fig 28   Ball position chart.

Neither should you be tempted, in general play, to push the hands ahead of the ball at address. I am aware that this is seen and used as a device to get the player to lead the clubhead into the ball on the downswing. During my golf clinics I demonstrate the fallacy of this theory by showing how moving the hands forward creates more problems than it solves. Although it has vital uses in the short game and for special shots, it has no place in the long game, nor in the method you are learning.

The Ball

However tempting it is to *hit* the ball, remember that ceding to this impulse can ruin your swing! Actually, the ball can often destroy your swing if you hypnotize yourself into staring at it.

In simple terms, the 'head-down, eye-on-the-ball' obsession cannot, and does not, improve technique. How can it? Usually, it preoccupies the mind to the extent that all you are thinking about is keeping your head down and eye on the ball, to the exclusion of other vital parts of the swing.

> **KEY POINT**
> Remember to keep your head *up*, not down, when you swing.

This philosophy was developed to ensure that your head stays still, but the head has no business being down. Indeed, the Professional Golf Association (PGA) Teaching Manual outlaws this advice. Have you ever seen a professional with his head down? Of course not. Professionals don't do it and neither should you. You should, however, know where your head is during the swing.

Observe your swing in a mirror, making sure that the head stays in the same spot in the mirror as you move from position to position throughout the swing. The

Fig 29   The best way to hold your partner's head still while practising.

Fig 30   A more painful alternative!

alternative is for your teacher or friend to hold your head by placing a hand on either side of it as you swing, releasing it after impact so you can turn to watch the flight of the ball.

A more painful alternative, one used by Jack Nicklaus's teacher, is to have someone grab a handful of your hair as you swing. You will soon know if your head is moving excessively!

CHAPTER 8

THE GOLF SWING COMPONENTS

The Takeaway

I have said that most swing errors can be traced to a faulty set-up or address. The other major area from which bad swings originate is in the takeaway. The takeaway is the first twelve to eighteen inches (thirty to forty-five centimetres) that the club travels at the start of the swing. If that is not right, the rest of the swing will be put out of focus. I could list a multitude of errors which occur frequently, but I would like you to concentrate on the correct way to start the club back and to fix it indelibly in your mind.

First refer briefly to the swing plane (*see* Chapter 12), the path around which the club must travel if you are to play consistently straight shots. For the moment we are concerned only with the first part of this plane (*see* Fig 58(a), darker blue area).

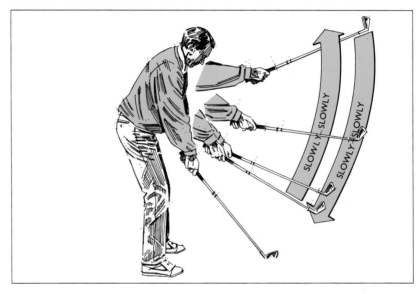

Fig 31   The arms, hands, and club move as one unit.

Practice Exercise

Select a no. 5 iron and take your address position, making sure your set-up is correct. (The proper takeaway can only be performed when your body is in the proper starting position.) Ensure that the ball is in the middle of your stance and ground your club behind it with the leading edge square, at right angles to the line flight. Make sure that the centre of the clubface is directly behind the ball.

    Now lift the club from the shoulders two or three times to get the feel of moving the arms, hands and club as one unit. Note that the wrists remain passive. This is a training exercise only and not used during general play.

    Return the clubhead to the ground behind the ball. Now move the clubhead back from the ball, ensuring that you

do not lose the relationship between the arms, hands and shaft. Note too that the wrist angle is maintained. (Fig 32 shows Nick Faldo doing just that, but with a driver. The technique is the same.)

    To help you get the right feel, imagine that your left elbow is being pushed back as if to start a péndulum in motion. There should be absolutely no resistance from your right arm; it should give way passively.

    The shoulders do not cause the arms to move: they move in response to the swinging of your arms. Remember, you have already demonstrated that your arms can move separately from your shoulders by moving them upwards in front of you several times. Do not dismiss the importance of this concept. It will enable you to establish a smooth start to your swing.

Fig 32   Nick Faldo – the takeaway.
Arms, hands and club working as one unit.

Fig 33   Ensure that the shoulders turn and do not tilt.

KEY POINT
Your shoulders should begin to respond by turning, not tilting or dipping.

You will see that the path of the club is in a slight inward curve. This is the beginning of the plane of the swing. It must not be exaggerated by taking it back too sharply. Nor should there be any effort to push the club back. Just *swing* it back.

Note also that no other part of the body moves during this process, particularly the left knee. I mention this because it is frequently taught that the left knee should fold in to point behind the ball at this stage. You may be tempted to experiment by trying it. Don't!

Take a look at some great golfing masters in the first stage of the correct swing and you will see that they do not immediately fold in their left knee. Note also the relationship of arm, wrist and shaft. These players are the ones to copy. In the light of this evidence some players still prematurely collapse the left knee inwards. Amongst other things this encourages the dropping of the left shoulder during the takeaway, which then leads to a multitude of other faults.

Your takeaway movement should be performed at least twice before proceeding to take the club back further; that is, take the club back 12–18in (30–45cm) and return it to the back of the ball, centring it in the middle of the blade until this can be done with ease and accuracy.

Practice Exercise

Here is another exercise, one you can perform without a club. It will enable you to get the feel and direction of the correct takeaway.

Simply extend your left hand in front of you, pointing your fingers at the ball. Now move your arm backwards about 6–9in (15–20cm) and return it to the original spot. Note the natural path your arm takes, and that your arm moves separately from your body. At the same time, the right shoulder also responds by turning and moving back laterally, not dipping down towards the ball.

Fig 34   The left arm traces the first
part of the takeaway.

swing. It is also the technique of learning to
recognize or know where the club is at all
times throughout the swing. This is rarely
given priority, especially on the downswing
and particularly in the finish.

Many major problems can occur when a
golfer is ignorant of club line technique. If
something goes wrong in the swing of a
'natural' player, the fault is difficult to
detect because this player is usually
ignorant of where the club should be
during the swing. Likewise, the long-

established high handicapper is never sure
where the club should be at any time, and
few even think that it matters. The
majority have a mental block from the
beginning to the end of their action.

Fig 35   Sandy Lyle – notice the controlled wrists, the balance and poise.

Now pick your club up again and try to
get the same feeling of separation of arm
and body. This cannot happen if the club is
held too tightly, so check your grip
pressure before starting.

This is the takeaway in its simplest and
purest form. However, I have yet to meet
a struggling player who is able to perform
the takeaway in the manner described
above. Usually it is hindered by too much
tension or excessive wrist action.

The hacker frequently dismisses this
part of the swing, or tries something
weird, new or contrived in order to get a
result. Do not fall into this habit. Get the
address position and the takeaway spot-on.

The Follow-Through

It may seem odd to be teaching you the
follow-through at this early stage. I prefer
to call it radical!

The Finish and Club Line

By starting at the finish you will immediately
become conscious of the role of the arms
and, more importantly, become aware of
the importance of the 'club line'.

The club line is the exact path on which
the club should travel throughout the

Thorough and correct training of my students ensures that they always know where the club should be throughout the swing. More importantly, they understand the technique of how to put it into each position. Let that be your aim too!

So, club line begins at the *finish* and gives you a re-introduction to arm swing and leverage within the compass of the golf swing itself.

It is very important that you visualize and copy this position precisely. It is important to note that there has been little or no movement in the wrists; arms have bent slightly from the elbow; and the upper arms are not against the body. Sandy Lyle, winner of two major championships consistently demonstrates the value of a properly poised and balanced finish.

Your final job is now to return the club to midriff height and check the leading edge of the blade of the club, which should be vertical, exactly as it was when you started. The shaft should also point towards the target line. This will create the classic curve of the body at the conclusion of great players' swings. The body is balanced and poised, your back is straight and the club has not been swung 'off line'. Nor has the body risen up. (A good example is champion golfer Laura Davis.)

> **KEY POINT**
> The head remains still and your height constant during this entire exercise.

It is crucial that you train yourself to complete this position with ease. It is a fallacy to believe that a good finish 'just happens'. It is pure luck if it does, and that is too much of a risk to take with your golf swing. At first, the finish will feel awkward but you are developing your new golf 'muscles' and training your body to accept positions that only occur in the golf swing. Habits formed early will stay for life. If they are good habits, then you have every chance of becoming a class player.

You have already met this concept during your preparation exercises at address. Now we are going to take you one step further.

Fig 36   *Laura Davis – notice the straight back and on-line finish to a powerful swing.*

Figs 37 (a)–(e)   The club line.

Fig 37 (a)   Address the ball on a tee peg.

Fig 37 (b)   The first eighteen inches of the backswing.

Fig 37 (c)   As the club swings past, move the knee inwards and come on to the point of the toe.

Practice Exercise

Place a ball on a tee, assume your address position and perform the first 18in of the backswing. As the clubhead changes direction to return to the ball, move the right knee inwards and roll onto the instep of the right foot, at the same time feeling a weight shift onto the outside of the left foot.

The club is now swinging slowly towards the target and being lifted by the arms and not the body. The ball will have travelled only a few yards. It is not the intention or purpose of this exercise to hit it further.

During this exercise, the right foot continues to move until it is balanced on the toe. At the same time, the hips and upper body gradually turn to face the target. The arms, meantime, continue to carry the club towards the intended line of flight to the finish position.

Fig 37 (d)   Let the club continue to swing slowly, lifted by the arms . . .

Fig 37 (e)   . . . until you reach your final balanced finish, with your weight now on your left side.

Fig 38   Scott Verplank. This type of flat, round finish is best left to the advanced player.

Fig 39   US Champion golfer Jan Stephenson. A bowed-back finish could lead to spine damage for the average golfer.

Practice Exercise

To further emphasize and consolidate your trained finish, do the following arm exercise while holding this final position.

Lift your arms up and down but with no wrist movement. The purpose of this exercise is to strengthen the forearms and to learn to control the wrists. I term it a vital 'freeing-up' exercise.

As a beginner, please beware of trying to emulate the full finish of some tournament players.

> **STAR TIP**
> *Mirror your back and through swings for consistency.*
>   Jose Maria Olazabal

It is even less advisable to copy the ones that have a 'round' or flat finish. Some players go for the back breaker. This frequently leads to back problems and should be avoided.

Beginners and struggling handicap players often try to copy their heroes in this respect, which is why they sometimes literally throw themselves off their feet.

Once you have learnt the correct finish,

Fig 40   A 'shoulders round' finish. Do not copy this one!

you may take a few liberties and add some professional touches, provided that you always return to the basic concept of a compact, controlled model finish on the practice area.

Once you get the feeling of the correct movement, check it out in a mirror from two angles. Work hard to master this vital exercise; it is the key to your future progress.

Remember to do the movements slowly. Try not to throw your upper body into it, otherwise you could end up with your shoulders spinning over your feet. That will never bring consistent results.

Work hard to achieve a balanced, on-line finish.

> **KIT CHECK**
> Golf shoes are essential for good footwork.

Fig 41   A model swing. The leading edge of the blade should be upright and point towards the target line.

CHAPTER 9

THE BACKSWING – A UNIQUE APPROACH

Before commencing the work outlined in this chapter, you should ensure that you can perform the front swing exercise to perfection. It is also a good idea to review your address position and set-up. Like the forward swing, the backswing relies on balance and poise.

You should already be able to perform the takeaway with reasonable ease and precision. The backswing is merely a continuation of the takeaway.

First, you must understand the true purpose of the backswing, which may not be as obvious as you think. Most players believe that the sole purpose of the backswing is to produce power. Traditional teaching does nothing to allay this concept. Most instruction books are littered with phrases such as 'winding up the body against the legs', 'activating the strength of the back muscles' and 'uncoiling like a spring', to name but a few. You must ignore these phrases if you are to reach your true potential.

> **KEY POINT**
> The true purpose of the backswing is to position the club.

The trained backswing is an effortless exercise which ensures that the club and body are positioned in such a way that power can be generated at the proper time: *at impact*. After all, you do not hit the ball with your backswing. The strike comes

Figs 42 (a)–(c) The backswing.

Fig 42 (a)   Start the takeaway with the hands, arms and club. Let the shoulders and hips respond.

Fig 42 (b)   Half way back.

Fig 42 (c)   The club has been carried to the top of the backswing by the left arm, with the hips level.

much later in the swing action and will be explained when we deal with the downswing.

So, let us go through the technique of how to achieve an effortless backswing.

Address the ball with a no. 5 iron, ensuring that your posture is perfect. Make sure that your arms are free to swing by lifting them up and down in front of you. You cannot do this simple pre-swing routine often enough!

Perform your takeaway, making sure that your hands, arms and club move as one unit (see Fig 31, page 39). You should feel your shoulders turning and your right hip beginning to draw back as you do so.

Continue to swing your arms back from the ball until your shoulders have nearly reached a full turn. By this stage, the butt end of the shaft will be pointing at your midriff, with the toe of the club pointing straight up towards the sky. Signs that your body is responding to the turn will be indicated by a slight lifting of the left heel and a 55 per cent weight shift on to the right leg. Your left knee will also be pointing slightly towards the ball.

At this stage, you should feel well balanced and ready to carry the club to the top of the backswing. This is simply a process of lifting the club upwards, using mainly your left arm. At the same time, you must have a distinct feeling of pushing the hips down, particularly the right hip.

KEY POINT
You must always ensure that the hips stay level.

In the completed backswing, your shoulders will have turned a full 90 degrees and the hips 45 degrees. You will notice that the line across your back appears to be leaning away from the ball. (This is as it should be.) Your right elbow will be pointing downwards, but will have moved away from the body. Make no attempt to pin this limb to your body.

Fig 43 Notice that the angle across the back is away from the ball.

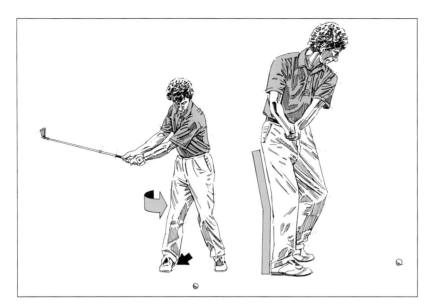

Fig 44   *The right knee must remain flexed and kinked inwards.*

KEY POINT
Throughout your action, you should think *swing*, not *hit*.

During this frequently used training exercise you will inevitably be letting your wrists move the clubhead too soon and use too much body action in an effort to get the club moving.

One of the best swings in the world at the time of writing belongs to big hitting Ian Woosnam, whose consummate ease when striking the ball should be a lesson to all those who think they have to hit the ball as hard as possible to get distance. Woosnam's economic action is a good model to copy.

Let us now review the points of our backswing;

1. Start from the correct address position.
2. Free the arms. Remember that exercise? Do it!
3. Start the takeaway with the hands, arms and shaft as one unit, with the shoulders turning in response.
4. At the halfway stage, check that the butt end of the club points towards your midriff, the toe of the club points upwards, the shoulders have almost fully turned and the right hip is drawn back.
5. Continue to carry the club to the top, using mainly left arm leverage, and make a complete 90 degrees shoulder turn.
6. The hips should be 'down' and level.
7. The right knee should be flexed inward.
8. The left heel should be up slightly, and the left knee pointed marginally behind the ball.
9. Your weight should be 55 per cent on the right leg and the body balanced and poised.
10. The shaft of a no. 5 iron should be slightly laid off but on plane, with the leading edge pointing at the target. The left wrist should be slightly 'cupped', and the right elbow pointing down.

You will see that there is a lot of checking to do! During your practice routine use a mirror or a video to confirm your positions.

Your body has turned in its own circle around your spine, with no semblance of tilt or sway. You may check this by ensuring that the right knee remains kinked inwards.

Another feeling you may well get is that the right side of your body has been drawn back to make room for the swing of the arms and club.

The position of the club at the top with a no. 5 iron will appear to be laid off, pointing to the right of the target. However, it is important to note that the leading edge is pointing *at* the target. You should also note that the wrist is slightly cupped and the shaft is still on the proper plane, that imaginary inclined circle around which the club must travel.

Only when a driver or fairway wood is used does the shaft point directly at the target. Do not attempt to point the shaft of the short irons in that direction. This leads to technical problems such as overswinging or crossing the line at the top, in which the club points to the right of target.

So far, you have been asked to perform the backswing in stages. You are not yet ready to swing at speed from the address position to the top. Before you make any attempt to do this, it is important to become aware of where the club is at each stage of your action, to sense where the clubhead is throughout the swing. You are getting used to manipulating 'the

instrument'. So go through your positional stages until you can achieve them with reasonable accuracy. A typical rush job is to swing the club back and forth, 'Just to get used to it'. This is no way to learn a precision move.

Fig 45   *This position is known as crossed line at the top – and is to be avoided.*

CHAPTER 10

THE DOWNSWING

You are now balanced and poised at the top of your backswing. The first instinct of the beginner is to start the downswing with a turn of the shoulders. This leads to numerous faults.

In an attempt to stop the shoulders initiating the downswing, the beginner will undoubtedly try to follow the traditional advice and start the downswing with a turn or a slide of the hips towards the target. The reasoning behind this popular theory is that the body will ultimately pull the arms and club through on the right line, thus creating power.

I firmly believe that it is harmful for a *beginner* to start the downswing in the above manner. Granted, tournament players often feel this is the correct way, and quite rightly so; this belief comes from the countless hours they spend hitting golf balls, during which they have developed terrific resistance in their legs, which then slide and turn in response to their intention to swing the club down and through.

Beginners should not attempt to start the downswing in the same way as a top player does, namely with the lower body. Results prove that this advice has failed miserably.

Downswing Priorities

The answer to the proper downswing lies in giving priority to the cultivation of an independent arm swing. Your first movement, therefore, must be to start your downswing with your left arm. It is swung downwards about 18in (45cm) without any movement from your shoulders.

Fig 46   The shoulders should never start the downswing.

Fig 47   *This is the correct way to practise the downswing.*

teaching your body to absorb feelings during each part of your swing movement, and retain them.

You are now half-way down and you have become aware that your hands and arms are swinging the club, but with your shoulders still fully turned. You are also aware of the resistance in your legs. Now is the time to lower your left heel to the ground and begin to move the right knee towards the target. This move will transfer the weight to the outside of your left leg which remains flexed. As the club continues its downward progression towards the back of the ball, let your hips slide and turn towards the target. This is helped by the action of your right foot now rolling inwards until it is balanced on the point of the right toe. The body movement during this part of the downswing is called the lower lateral shift, which is essential in helping to swing the club through to your trained balanced finish.

The downswing is a highly co-ordinated series of moves, so do not expect to grasp it immediately. The additional instructive exercises in the next chapter will help you to perfect it.

Fig 48   *Front view of a trained, balanced finish.*

This is the most crucial movement you will ever have to learn. To get the feel of this initial move, return the club to the top, pause, and repeat. Do this many times, maintaining your body poise but becoming aware of a developing upward resistance in your legs. Notice that this resistance happens as you start your downswing. It occurs because your body is preparing itself for what is to follow.

Provided that you are not holding the club too tightly, you will also be aware of the clubhead 'asking' to be used. To release it at this early stage would be premature, so you must maintain the angle between the wrists and the shaft. You are

CHAPTER 11

DOWNSWING EXERCISES

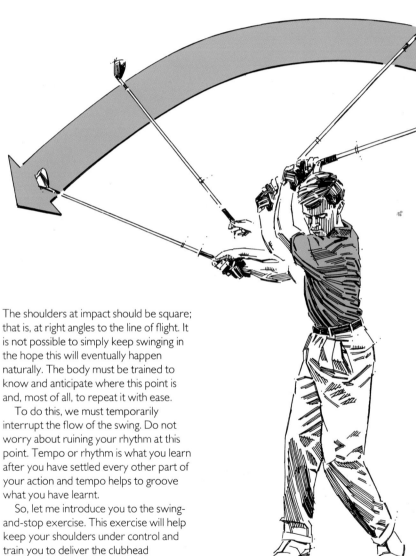

The shoulders at impact should be square; that is, at right angles to the line of flight. It is not possible to simply keep swinging in the hope this will eventually happen naturally. The body must be trained to know and anticipate where this point is and, most of all, to repeat it with ease.

To do this, we must temporarily interrupt the flow of the swing. Do not worry about ruining your rhythm at this point. Tempo or rhythm is what you learn after you have settled every other part of your action and tempo helps to groove what you have learnt.

So, let me introduce you to the swing-and-stop exercise. This exercise will help keep your shoulders under control and train you to deliver the clubhead accurately at the point of impact.

Please note that I have said 'deliver the

Fig 49   Fishing! The clubhead is released too early.

clubhead' not 'hit the ball'. The swing-and-stop routine will eliminate the desire to hit.

The Swing-and-Stop Exercise

Perform your backswing from your correct address position, remembering to commence with two short takeaways.

Pause once at the top of the swing, then bring the club down with the hands and arms at an even pace and in sequence of left arm, left heel down, right foot roll, hips sideways. Now stop the club at impact with your hands and with the clubhead totally square. You will notice that your body is positioned almost as it was at address, except that your right knee is in, your right heel off the ground and your weight shifted to the left. Your hips have turned slightly and, most importantly, your shoulders are square.

The shoulders stay passive. Note particularly the start of this action, where the right shoulder stays back and the angle between the wrists is maintained.

If the clubhead is swinging ahead of the arms, (this is called casting or fishing) then it will arrive ahead of the hands at impact and will be virtually impossible to stop at impact without hurting the left wrist. Equally, it will be totally impossible to

Figs 50 (a)–(d)   The hit-and-stop exercise.

Fig 50 (a)   Pause at the top of the swing.

Fig 50 (b)   Swing down – shoulders passive – wrist angle preserved.

Fig 50 (c)   Just before impact. The left heel has returned; right foot and knee in. The hips have moved laterally.

Fig 50 (d)   The club is stopped dead with the hands. The shoulders are square and the clubface too!

'square up' at impact if your shoulders turn first. The exercise is therefore excellent for controlling the upper part of the body.

At first, you will find it impossible to get everything exactly in the right place at the right time. That is the same with learning any set of precision moves, so practise patiently and do not apply too much pressure in the movement. Advanced students can actually 'drop and stop', meaning they have acquired the ability to feel the arms so free to swing down from the top that they can virtually let the arms free-fall into the space provided by the body and 'catch' the club at the bottom of the swing.

If effort was required by top players when striking irons, then they would not be capable of the phenomenal accuracy they achieve. Furthermore, the procedure of the swing-and-stop exercise enables players to strike the ball consistent distances with each club because at no time are they thinking 'hit'.

The swing-and-stop exercise will go some way to getting the feel of swinging the club and controlling your shoulders, but ultimately you have to become aware of 'left-side control'.

Left-Side Control

This means being able to produce a backhand stroke with your left arm. The benefit of this technique is that it further nullifies the natural overpowering tendencies of the right side of the body, the dominant side in all other ball games.

A dominant right side is one reason why natural ball-game players find it so hard to adapt to golf. They are used to throwing the overenthusiastic right shoulder, hand and arm into all their actions. Squash and badminton players have the additional problem of controlling an overactive wrist, the last thing required in golf swing technique.

Left-side control is necessary if you wish to advance beyond the middle handicap stage. It is an invaluable help if introduced as soon as you begin to make a reasonable swing outline. The left arm does what the

Fig 51   A dipped left shoulder and a rising right hip – one of the worst faults in golf.

right arm cannot achieve: it controls the radius of the swing and maps out the arc or plane.

The left hand also controls the angle of the wrist at the top, and, as explained, the left arm starts the downswing. It is also necessary to appreciate the levering effect of this arm so that it can carry the club from half-way to the top without interference from the right hand.

Right-hand interference is a frequent occurence with many players who simply change from the left to the right and then kill their swing on the way down with their strongest hand. Furthermore, if the left side (arm) is never strengthened or made properly aware of its role, then you will be forever plagued with a rising right hip and dipped left shoulder, which is in effect the right side doing what the left is incapable of. This is a common swing fault among handicap golfers.

Here are some exercises to train your left arm to swing.

Practice Exercise One

Take your correct address position with a no. 7 iron. Remove your right hand from the grip. Move your left arm level with your left side. Lever the club up and down with no movement of the wrist, but retain the exact angle as at address.

Do this slowly, swinging from the shoulder joint, and be aware of the support of your forearm muscles.

This exercise will also develop the all-important upper-arm leverage feel. During this, you will begin to feel your left arm working. Do not under any circumstances lift the body, as that will neutralize some of the effectiveness of the exercise. Repeat several times and do it as a reminder throughout your golfing life. Over a period of time, your left arm will learn to do its job.

Practice Exercise Two

Start as in the first exercise and go through the 'up the side of the body' motion two or three times. Return the club to the centre of the stance and ensure that both the grip and address position are perfect and particularly that your right shoulder is below your left. Perform your backswing with the left arm only! Keep your right arm as relaxed as possible, so that it is hanging down as you do so.

Figs 53 (a)–(h)
Left arm exercise.

Fig 53 (a)   Take the address position with your left arm only.

Fig 53 (e)   Starting down with the arm only – in perfect plane.

Fig 52   A left arm exercise to get the feeling of upper-arm leverage.

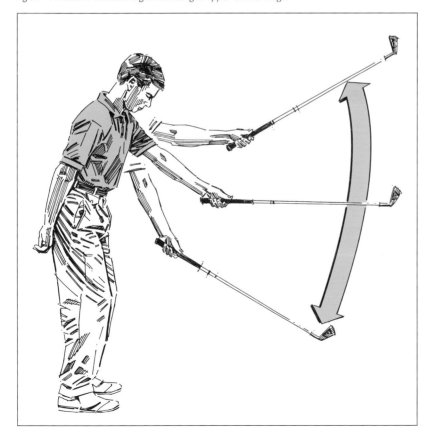

Fig 53 (b)   The club has started back as one unit. No wrists are involved.

Fig 53 (c)   Half way back: the same as a swing with both hands.

Fig 53 (d)   Top of swing stop. Note that hip and shoulders are drawn back.

Fig 53 (h)   At impact. The shoulders are square as is the clubface. The weight has been transferred via the feet and the left side has controlled the whole movement.

Fig 53 (f)   Hip height. The feet have moved into position.

Fig 53 (g)   Just before impact. Note: the right side is still passive.

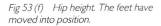

In the above exercise, you will be inclined to use your body to assist the backswing; that is, you will tend to drop the left shoulder and lift the right. Take great care to avoid falling into this trap.

Swing your arm at an even pace, ensuring that the same exacting half-way backswing position is achieved during the club's progress to the top. On no account must you swing the club back aimlessly and swiftly, as this will encourage many faulty wrist angles and other wrong moves.

Fig 54   A balanced finish – the result of a proper downswing.

Initially, your arm will wilt under the weight. Do not worry; this is natural and goes to show just how weak your arm was in the first place! You can alleviate some of the strain at first by choking down on the grip. (Go down to the steel shaft if necessary.) Later, you can return to the full length as your arm becomes stronger.

When you first practise this exercise, you may not be able to get your arm as high as it will ultimately have to go, but work at it each day. A few minutes is all the time required.

Now to the downswing. It is not necessary to swing down and *through*. We merely want you to get the feel of the left arm by swinging down slowly, tracing and controlling the exact line to the ball. The club must stay behind the hands or 'in plane' during this motion. This is much harder than you think and will be explained in more detail when we deal more fully with the plane of the swing in Chapter 12.

It is important to note that throughout this one-armed action, the technique is the same as for the two-arm swing. The body responds in the same way: namely, arm first, leg action, lateral weight-shift and exact impact position with the blade absolutely square. If that seems difficult, remember that if you want to be good, you have to expect to work for it; so keep at it.

Practice Exercise Three

This is a very easy exercise, done without a club. The benefit is that it can be done anywhere and any time. So there is no excuse for not practising!

Start from the address position. Although you are not using a club, ensure that your posture is as it would normally be: chest and head up, stomach in, bottom back and knees flexed.

Now simply extend your left arm in front of you as if you were holding a club, except that your hand should be open, with the back of the hand to the target and fingers pointing to where the ball would be.

of total freedom with no interference from your right side. This is an invaluable aid to understanding how little the right side is felt during the swing of a first-class player.

The majority of players go through their golfing life never experiencing the left side controlling the swing. They know only right-side dominance. The feel of the correct swing is so totally different. It takes a lot of re-training of every instinct for the handicap golfer to make a complete transition, but the results are worth the effort. The swing will flow with much more ease and consistency.

The Swing Shape Without a Club

This exercise was invented by the renowned golf teacher, Leslie King. It is done without a club, and by learning it thoroughly you will be able to maintain your swing shape forever.

Concentrate totally on body position, poise and arm swing. You can perform this exercise anywhere and use it as a blue print if you like. Refer to it if things go wrong: it will never let you down.

Take your correct position without a club. Grasp your left wrist gently and swing your arms up and down in front of you to free them.

Start your movement with your left hand and arm, swinging it back on its natural arc while your shoulders turn in response. Continue by drawing your right hip back, at the same time lifting the left heel slightly, feeling pressure on the big toe joint. Keep your right knee flexed and do not sway.

At the half-way point, the shoulders should be turned 90 degrees and the hips 45 degrees. Your arm should be extended at right angles to the shoulders. Continue to lift the left arm to the top of the swing, noting the angle of the wrist and thumb which should be pointing towards the target.

Swing the left arm down about 12–18in (30–45cm), but do not move any other part of your body at this stage, particularly

Fig 55   Practise this exercise to cultivate the feeling and line of the downswing.

Perform the backswing with your left arm only, positioning your hand properly at the top.

Hold your backswing position intact and swing your left arm down and across your chest and back up again, still maintaining your body in a backswing poise. Repeat frequently.

During this exercise you will get a feeling

Fig 56 (a)   Take your address position without a club and grasp your left wrist gently.

Fig 56 (b)   Start your movement with your left hand and arm. The right shoulder begins to respond.

Fig 56 (c)   Half way back: shoulders and hips turned, left heel up nearly at the top.

Fig 56 (g)   Waist height: feet, hips (lateral shift) active; shoulders controlled.

Fig 56 (h)   Impact. Shoulders square, hips beginning to turn to target.

Fig 56 (i)   The body now 'opens' to allow the arms to swing towards the target.

Fig 56 (d)   Top of swing. The body is fully coiled: left arm leverage.

Fig 56 (e)   In evidence: thumb pointing at target.

Fig 56 (f)   The left arm drops (swings) down while the body stays fully turned.

Fig 56 (j)   The weight is now on the left side as the arms continue to swing.

Fig 56 (k)   The finished position, balanced and poised.

your head and the right shoulder. Do not lose height. Respond now with your legs by putting the left heel down and the right knee in towards the target. Continue to swing the arm down and across the chest. At the same time, slide the hips to the left (lateral shift) and come up on the ball of the right foot.

At the impact position, the shoulders should be square with your weight on the left foot and hands back at address position. Continue to sweep the arms towards the target, while the hips turn and the leg action is completed. Your body now faces the target, the back straight, the right leg folded in and balanced on the point of the right toe, with your hands beside the left ear.

KEY POINT
This exercise contains the very essence of your swing shape. Learn to do it to perfection.

CHAPTER 12

THE SWING PLANE

I have left teaching the plane of the swing until now because it causes more confusion than any other part of the swing. That it should be such a difficult concept to grasp is strange, because it appears simple when you see the imaginary circle around which the club should travel (*see* Fig 57).

I trace a lot of the confusion to the well-meaning description of golf swing which states that 'You take the club round your body on the backswing, bring it back on the inside to straight, then round on the finish.'

I agree that this is precisely the path the club takes, but to describe it in that form has led to more slicers and hookers than straight-hitters!

The problem seems to lie in implanting the word 'round' into the mind of a beginner or struggling golfer, because the natural tendency is to go *round* anyway (most times from the shoulders downwards).

So, let us take a fresh look at the problem of getting the club to swing 'round' the plane of the swing without mentioning that word!

Fig 57   The plane of the swing – try to visualize this as you practise.

Performing the Swing Plane

The plane should normally be related to the height of the individual. For the purposes of our instruction we will stick to an average height.

Before you can hope to maintain a good plane, you must have a good-shaped swing along the lines described in this book. A poor backswing totally cancels any hope of performing a proper swing plane. If in doubt, have a polaroid taken of your backswing. If it in any way resembles the picture on page 53, you are best advised to correct your position by referring to the earlier chapters and then to come back to this point!

You must have control of the club to learn to swing consistently on plane. That is another reason why, when teaching a beginner, I do not tackle the subject in depth until a reasonable degree of stability in body poise and arm movements is achieved.

We will assume that you now have that qualification, so let us delve into the workings of the swing plane and learn to stay on the right plane.

So, how do we perform the proper plane? Because the plane is a crucial element of the swing, we will take it in stages.

Figs 58 (a) and (b)   The swing plane, stage one.

Fig 58 (a)   The takeaway – the first part of the plane.

Fig 58 (b)   At the top of the swing, both the wood and the iron are 'in plane'.

Stage One

Start in the correct address position using a mid-iron, tee the ball up on a high peg. Now, swing the club to the half-way back position. Notice how the clubhead has traced out the first part of the plane. This was done by sticking to our established technique of swinging the club, wrist and arm together, while making a natural turn of the body.

The next move is to lift the club upwards with the left arm, at the same time allowing the club to find the upper part of the plane. With an iron it appears 'laid off'; with a wood, the shaft points directly down the target line.

Stage Two

Hand-Line Training

With the club properly positioned at the top of the backswing, drop the arms directly downwards for about 12–18in (30–45cm), letting the left arm control the action. At this stage, the shoulders remain fully turned. Note how the club naturally traces out the first part of the downswing plane, which will appear flatter than the upswing. It is at this point that you arrange your body for the next series of moves. Your left heel goes down and your right knee kicks in, the right heel comes off the

Figs 59 (a)–(e)   The swing plane, stage two.

Fig 59 (a)   *Drop the club and arms to about half-way, keeping the shoulders fully turned.*

Fig 59 (b)   *Maintain the club as in Fig 59 (a), but set your lower body to new position.*

ground and your hips slide slightly towards the target, with the weight on the left foot.

Do not alter the position of your arms or the club because they are perfectly positioned for the next part of your hand-line training.

The shaft should now be pointing towards the ball. Even so, the temptation will be great to move the head of the club 'to get it straight'.

Because the blade faces outwards at this point, you may fear that the ball will veer off at right angles unless something is done to bring the club face square. Any attempt to manipulate the club in this way will force it out of plane, resulting in either a slice or pulled shot.

The squaring-up process will happen naturally if it is allowed to. The answer is to 'see' the release of the clubhead as illustrated.

This is very much a downward movement, a combination of arm swing and hand action. It is learned by letting the clubhead approach the ball in increments, while the sensitive hands gently feel the build-up caused naturally by the weight of the clubhead. This is very slight, because you are going slowly. Under the pressure of a half or full swing, this feeling is more intense.

Note also how the clubhead appears to be open until the very last moment. Do

Fig 59 (c)   It is now crucial that the club should continue downwards and 'in plane'.

Fig 59 (d)   Lower the club in stages through this area to train your hands to recognize the positions.

Fig 59 (e)   The club continues through to an on-line finish.

not lose your nerve! The natural recovery of your hands and body will 'square it up' and the momentum will carry the club towards the target with the blade square. There is absolutely no need to 'close' the blade, it *will* square up if you let it.

After impact, your trained leg and hip action will allow you to continue to swing the club through to an 'on line' finish. Notice how at the front end of the plane the shaft lies in the opposite and complementary angle. Make no attempt to throw the club over the other way.

Let me stress that this is a highly delicate series of manœuvres and requires the utmost concentration to achieve success.

Pictures and text are poor substitutes for a three-dimensional image, but they hopefully give you a good idea of the procedure.

Observe the picture of Greg Norman's swing from front on. It shows the approach of the clubhead on plane to the ball. This, combined with the exercise just described, should help you to unravel the mysteries of the swing plane.

The next step is to put it together as a swing, but do not hurry on to this next stage until you can perform the previous exercise with a degree of understanding and skill.

Fig 60   Greg Norman approaching the ball on a perfect plane.

Figs 61 (a)–(c)   The swing plane, stage three.

Fig 61 (a)   Swing the club down to about half-way and pause.

Fig 61 (b)   Work the arms easily up and down, maintaining the club 'in plane', . . .

Fig 61 (c)   . . . releasing it through the impact area to a controlled finish.

Stage Three

As in the first stage, take your address position with a five iron and the ball on a tee. This time, swing the club to the top with an even, unhurried tempo, being aware as you do so of the various positional elements. From the top of the swing, start your next movement with a downward swing of your left arm as already described, but pause in the half-way down position.

You must feel balanced, poised and be looking ahead mentally to visualize the feel of your trained lower-body action as it would normally continue. You are now going to concentrate solely on swinging and releasing the clubhead through its last vital journey into the back of the ball without losing plane, releasing the clubhead as you do by keeping the 'swing' in your arms, and sensitivity in your hands. There should be absolutely no tightness in your body as this will lock the wrists. To maintain the impetus and flow of your arm swing, move the club up and down (see Fig 61 (b)). A few inches is enough to alert the body that the club is about to swing through on the same path as it did (by increments) previously.

When you feel ready to have a go at the final delivery stage, simply let the left hand and arm control the final stage, making sure you allow the clubhead to release downwards into the back of the ball. At the same time, your body will respond by continuing its lower lateral shift-and-turn, assisting the club through to an 'on line' compact finish.

Your initial concern will be that the ball go to the right, because the angle of the approach is across and parallel to the turned shoulder-line. Do not worry, your body is in the process of squaring up. (This, in itself, is enough to compensate for what appears to be a drastic approach from the 'inside'.) It is quite likely that the ball will fly slightly to the right. However, this could indicate that you are on the right line, but that your hands have not learned to relax sufficiently to time a square delivery of the clubhead.

The proper delivery will happen with practice and you will begin to feel very clearly that the left arm and the back of the wrist simply *lead* the clubhead through the ball. When you do achieve this on-plane, in-line delivery, the feeling will be unmistakable. The ball will seem 'soft' on the blade and will travel a long way with little physical effort. You will then appreciate how and why the pros play with such consummate ease!

CHAPTER 13

THE SECRET OF POWER

I will give odds that you have turned to this page first, such is the fascination exerted by power, and the priority it is given in the minds of golfers. Most can think of nothing else but getting that ball out there a long way.

It has been stated, and proved, that any player who can only hit the ball 150yd, but does so accurately, will break 80 every time. But this is not what the average golfer wants to hear.

So, for what it's worth, here is how controlled power is generated and how it can be developed.

Generating Power

First, get it out of your mind that the shoulders are in some way involved. Remember, fully turned shoulders on the backswing simply enable you to *position* the club, ready for the downswing. Neither are the legs in themselves a *direct* source of power. Resistance and counterforce are the keys to power.

> **KEY POINT**
> Power is created by *resistance* and *counterforce*.

Fig 62   Ian Woosnam, reputed for the power he imparts into his shots.

Counterforce cannot be felt and anticipated until you become aware, either consciously or unconsciously, of the swing of your arms against the resistance in your legs that indicates the potential power to be delivered finally with your hands. The ability to achieve this is not an overnight occurrence, and those who try to hurry the process only manage to push themselves further down the road to the hackers' graveyard!

As a class player swings to the top of his backswing, there will be a feeling of resistance in the legs. This is instrumental in keeping the shoulders firmly under control. It also allows the player to lever the left arm upwards without the body rising. This is termed upward resistance.

The player now starts the downswing with the left arm. The left heel is then returned immediately to the ground. It in turn triggers an instant response in the

lower body, which will move to the left. This is the *lateral shift* which sets up a resistance momentarily in the left leg. It also has the function of keeping the shoulders under control. The club is now half-way

> **STAR TIP**
> To hit the ball further, think 'Swing' and not 'Hit'.
>   Ian Woosnam

Figs 63 (a)–(g)   The 'power' sequence.

Fig 63 (a)   Club positioned at the top
– resistance is felt in the legs.

Fig 63 (b)   The left arm starts the
downswing triggering instant response
in the lower body.

Fig 63 (c)   As the arm continues
down, a lateral shift occurs. (The
shoulders are still under control.)

down and the angle between the wrist is maintained.

At this instant, too, the right foot comes into play and the heel will rise. This now takes on the resistance role as the hands begin to release the clubhead towards the ball. It kicks in really fast to consolidate the backward resistance, just prior to impact, as the hands commence their task of releasing the clubhead.

At impact, the right heel is up and the knee has folded in towards the left: you have applied force with your hands and arms against the resistance of the lower body in a trained and organized manner.

Just after impact, the resistance is transferred to the small of the back which sets up a counterforce against which to swing the club through towards the target for an on-line, balanced finish.

This series of moves occurs subconsciously and spontaneously in top players. They were beginners once, however, and a beginner cannot expect that level of technical performance until he has gone through an intense period of training, during which each step of creating 'power' will become clear.

There is no short-cut, so be patient. It is worth the wait.

Fig 63 (d)   Impact! Shoulders square
– hips clearing.

Fig 63 (e)   Only now does the body begin to turn towards the target.

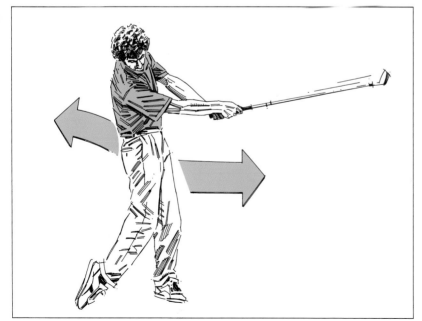

Fig 63 (f)   The hands and arms swing the club towards the target.

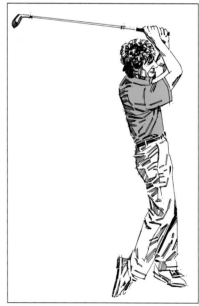

Fig 63 (g)   A perfectly balanced
on-line finish.

CHAPTER 14

PUTTING IT ALL TOGETHER – AND CHECKING IT OUT

There comes a time when you must link everything you have learned together to make your swing one complete movement. At the early stages, this is where things go 'wrong'. This is inevitable and is the prime reason why no player can ever be his own teacher – no matter what his standard. A beginner will need an expert eye continually correcting and re-adjusting – in effect, coaching the player. Ideally, this process should continue for at least a year.

KEY POINT

It is futile for the beginner to try to improve without any assistance, in the form of a coach or teacher, *unless* he has a clear idea of what shape he is intending to make.

In this book, I have repeated a specific swing shape (call it a model or a blueprint), so that you can fix this model in your mind. You can then check your positions in a mirror, or video your swing and use the still-frame facility to compare your positions with those of our model swingers.

It is particularly difficult to maintain your 'shape' at first. Nevertheless, you must attempt to do so.

Swing Model Review

1. Take your correct position at the ball. Check your alignment carefully.
2. Place the clubhead behind the ball.
3. Perform two short 'takeaways'.
4. Make a smooth backswing, ensuring

that your body turns and positions itself in response to the swing of your arms.
5. Position the club at the top and *pause*.

6. Commence your downswing with your left arm, *downwards*, keeping your 'plane' exercise in mind.

Figs 64 (a)–(c), Figs 65 (a)–(c) and Figs 66 (a)–(c)   These sequences illustrate uniformity of swing shape.

(a)

7. Swing through the impact area to a balanced and controlled finish.
8. Note that we have ignored the ball! Too much concentration on that object can lead to a mistimed delivery.

If you are using video, check the results on screen and compare them with the swing models described in previous chapters. Do your check in this order:

1. Address: is it *absolutely* correct?
2. Finish: is this per our models?

3. Takeaway: did your wrists 'whip' the clubhead too quickly or out of line? Check the half-way back position.
4. At the top:
   a) Are you in plane?
   b) Have you overswung with your iron?
   c) Are you either 'cross-line' or overlaid off?
   d) Is your blade square?
5. On the downswing:
   a) Did your shoulders start first?
   b) Did the shaft move out of plane?
   c) Did you 'throw' the clubhead first

instead of leading it down in plane behind the hands?
6. At impact:
   a) Are you flat-footed? Check your lateral shift.
   b) Are your shoulders square?

KEY POINT
Attention to detail is the hallmark of champions. Remember that golf is a precision game!

(b)

(c)

(a)

(b)

(c)

(a)

(b)

(c)

PART 3
THE SHORT GAME

CHAPTER 15

BASIC SHOTS

Instruction in this section will be kept as simple as possible. As a beginner, it would be unwise to try to master the hundreds of finesse shots available to top players. You will be wasting valuable time trying to cope with shots you are technically ill-equipped to attempt.

> **KEY POINT**
> The nearer you get to the green, the narrower your stance and the closer you will be to the ball.

Instead, I shall give you fundamental advice to cope with the basic shots to get you on the green and somewhere near the flag. Practice and experience will in time do the rest.

The casual player's most common fault is to use the normal set-up and usual swing, causing him to decelerate the club at impact. The result is either a 'fat' or 'thinned' shot.

One basic rule is: never start your swing with your wrists. Swing with your *arms* and eliminate practically all wrist break. This advice comes from the highest level: five times Open Champion and renowned short-game expert, Tom Watson. It also closely follows the system you are learning from this book. (Only on certain shots should the wrists consciously come into play.)

Because I recommend limited use of the wrists does not mean that you should have stiff wrists. It means *controlled* wrists and holding the club lightly in the fingers. The way to control your wrists is to learn to swing your arms freely. If your arms cannot move, your wrists must!

Understanding this concept will make all the difference between success and failure.

Fig 67   The set-up for chipping.

Chipping

Chipping is like putting with a lofted club, say a no. 8 iron, and should be used from about 20yd (18m) from the flag. The object is to hit the ball forward and let it roll, relying on the loft of the club to get the ball airborne. Hence, the 'chip-and-run'. You may select any club from a wedge to a five iron for this purpose.

The Set-Up for Chipping

1. Place your feet close together.

2. Open your stance by about 10 degrees, so that a line across the toes would be pointing left of the target.
3. Place your hands slightly forward.
4. Choke down on grip.
5. Move the weight towards the left leg.

Reasons

1. Placing your feet close together restricts body movement.
2. An open stance gives the club an easier path to the target.
3. Placing the hands forward means that they will lead the clubhead through the ball.

Fig 69   Collapsed left wrist – a common chipping fault.

Fig 68   On the backswing use very little wrist action: swing the arms.

4. Choking down on the club gives more control and crisper shots.
5. Weight on the left foot ensures that you will strike the ball first.

The Stroke

Backswing

Swing the club back with the left arm in control just past your right knee using a firm-wristed putting action. Let the shoulders turn a little in response. (This is identical to your usual takeaway but your hands started in a forward position.)

Downswing

Start back by leading, but swinging, the clubhead to and past the ball, again with the left arm. Swing to a brief finish with the blade on line to your target, allowing your right knee to fold in as the club passes by. The distance you swing back will equal the distance you swing through.

Try not to contrive this action. Hold the club lightly, so that you will learn to sense these things happening. It is vital that your left wrist does not 'collapse' at impact. If you have been working through the swing system in this book, and have practised both your left arm swing and the finish of your swing, you will have no problem controlling your left wrist after impact.

> **KEY POINT**
> 'Leading' means feeling the left wrist advancing first, with the clubhead following.

Another way to control the wrists is by adopting the putting grip, i.e. reverse overlap (*see* page 84). Some pros swear by it as an aid to keeping the wrists under control.

The Swing-Through

This is more a question of rhythm than anything else. You must practise your chipping stroke at every opportunity, even during a round while waiting between shots. Chip blades of grass or weeds, anything! Continuous practise leads to smoothness.

Many beginners are inclined to hit at the ball or to scoop it up rather than sweep through. This is a natural reaction getting the better of your intentions. You see the ball and want to hit it! This is really a case of 'ball fixation', so here is a good tip . . .

Place a tee peg 2in (50cm) in front of the ball and aim at it while swinging. This takes your concentration off the ball, so you will hit *through* the ball at the peg and the early hit disappears.

Tom Watson's short game skill is legendary and I picked up an excellent tip after watching him on several occasions.

When Tom is faced with a short chip, particularly from light rough, he makes his practice swings much longer than the actual swing he intends to use, accelerating as he does so. At first, I thought, 'If he hits it at that pace, he will clear the green and the crowd.' But no, as soon as he played his chip, it was back to the appropriate short swing and a perfect shot!

Having experimented with this, I realized that it was an excellent means of preventing freezing or quitting on a chip: it keeps the arms swinging, then, it is just a case of stepping up to the ball and letting

Fig 70   A tee peg in front helps to take your mind off hitting the ball!

them do the same, only using a shorter swing. This tip, of course, fits in well with our arm swing concept, so try it out when you are faced with that kind of pressure shot.

Once you have got the hang of the chipping stroke, practise it with various clubs from the wedge to the five iron, remembering to choke down for consistency. Observe and study the results.

For instance, you will obviously get far more run on the five iron than on the wedge. As a beginner, it will pay to keep the ball rolling with a low-numbered iron rather than the steep, lofted wedge.

Playing a high chip shot with an open-faced wedge requires much more skill because less face is presented to the ball. Consequently, you have more chance of 'thinning' it through the green.

When using your chipping technique in actual play, try to visualize how the ball

will react on its way to the hole. That means picking a spot and trying to land the ball on it.

The more accurate you get in this respect, the better your chances of holing a few shots from off the green.

Chipping is like a putting stroke, so never miss an opportunity to use your putter from just off the green – or even further away if the grass is cut short or the ground baked hard. You will have far more chance of getting close to the flag this way. This shot is known in the business as the 'Texas Wedge'.

> **KEY POINT**
> It pays to use the percentage game as often as possible in golf. No lesser player than five times Open Champion Tom Watson says that your best putt from off the green will always be more accurate than your best chip.

Pitching

A pitch is really a half swing, whereas a chip is an extended putt. You can pitch from any distance, from 50 yards down to as little as 5 yards. The pitch shot will always throw the ball high in the air, so that the ball will land softly and stop.

> **KIT CHECK**
> Your most useful pitching clubs are the pitching wedge, sand wedge, nine, eight and seven irons in that order.

Let us first deal with the basic pitching stroke intended to propel the ball 40–50yd (35–45m). For this exercise you will require a pitching wedge.

The Set-Up for Pitching

The set-up is identical to that for the chip, except that:
1. Your feet are placed slightly further apart.
2. The full length of the grip is utilized. (However, both these techniques may be modified for the shorter shots.)
3. Place your hands ahead of the ball.
4. Weight is shaded towards the left foot.
5. The ball is positioned in the centre of an open stance, that is with your feet facing left of the target line.

The Stroke

Backswing

The technique is similar to our half-way back position of the full swing, except that the wrists are a little more cocked, but no more than illustrated.

During the takeaway, remember to turn your body and not tilt, and to start the club back with the hands and arms as one unit, but with the left arm in charge as usual. The left heel is best kept down although a *slight* lift will do no harm.

Downswing

Simply return your hands and arms to the address position, keeping the club in plane and not forgetting your leg action; so

Fig 71   The set-up for the pitch shot.

Fig 72   The backswing for a pitch shot.

Fig 73   Through impact, wrists should be firm.

Fig 74   Pitch shot finish – brief and controlled.

let that right knee kick in. Lead the clubhead through with your left arm, ensuring that your left wrist does not collapse at impact. Finally, keep the club accelerating through to a brief, controlled finish.

Like the chipping stroke, the length of backswing should equal the length of the follow-through. In other words, keep it brief and crisp.

During your practice routine, hit shots at an even tempo, getting the feel of this new variation of the swing and notice how far the ball travels. This will give you an indication of your maximum distance. Learn to put this in your muscle memory because you can utilize this information to play the shorter shots with the same swing by choking down the grip in half-inch increments. As a general rule, you will reduce the distance by about 5yd per half-inch (4·5m per centimetre) without changing your swing action. At the early stage of your development, this knowledge will save you having to try to deliberately vary your swing for each shot.

Beginners and experienced week-end golfers are always fascinated by backspin, by those spectacular shots to the green that bite and suck back. This is purely a 'trick of the trade' demonstrated by an expert at his profession and best reserved for advanced players to experiment with.

My advice is to concentrate on a consistent, accurate strike that will produce enough controllable spin to stop the ball on any good green.

Many professionals play all their pitches with just one club, usually a sand wedge.

KEY POINT
Concentrate on the pitching wedge and get to know its capabilities. If struck properly, it should lift the ball high in the air at a consistent height.

Others have as many as three wedges in their bags with varying degrees of loft.

If you wish to vary the height to which the ball will fly, here is how . . .

The Low-Flying Wedge

Move the ball back in your stance, (see Fig 75) thus bringing the hands forward. This effectively de-lofts the club and sends the ball on a much lower trajectory. If your contact has been good, you will find the ball will stop surprisingly quickly.

The High Shot

Open your stance even more than usual and move the ball forward, level with your left heel. This will bring your hands in line with the ball and restore the full loft to your club. Play your normal swing, but use a little extra lateral shift (leg movement). This will help to slide the face of the club under the ball, producing a high shot with a soft landing. Do not expect a lot of distance from this shot. It is in effect a sliced wedge! It is similar in technique to the 'cut-up' or 'bunker' stroke.

This, then, is chipping and pitching in their simplest form.

Fig 75   For the low shot, position the ball back in your stance, hands forward.

CHAPTER 16

PUTTING – A GAME WITHIN A GAME

Many people believe that golf actually consists of two games. There is the game played in the air and the one played along the ground; namely, putting.

Once you start to play, you will soon realize that half the strokes in a round of golf are taken on the putting surface. There is absolutely no value in reaching the green in regulation, only to flounder and take three or four putts. You must acquire a good putting stroke.

It is ironic to think that a player can move a ball 450 yards in two shots and sometimes take three more to cover a mere 10 feet, but unfortunately it does happen!

Putting to the professional tournament player can make all the difference between success and obscurity – hence the almost neurotic quest on the part of professionals to find a putter or a method (or both) that will guarantee to see the ball directed with certainty to its final destination below ground.

> **STAR TIP**
> On long puts, concentrate on distance and getting close enough to make your next shot comparatively simple.
> Ian Woosnam

There is more to it than that. Putting requires not only delicacy of touch, but also total control of both nerves and mind so that vital putts are not missed under pressure.

No matter how sound the technique, a player must be able to control his hands during the putting stroke. Any deterioration of mind or body will manifest itself on the putting surface.

Fig 76   Bernhardt Langer. At first, he tried this putting grip . . .

The Putting Advantage

Putting is the one area in which amateurs have a real opportunity to be as good as the professionals. In fact many amateurs are, and they need to be because their long game may be so flawed that the green is their only chance of salvation!

The putting stroke is the simplest of actions and relatively easy to learn because excessive force is not required and there is no body action to learn. Furthermore, it is a highly individual stroke. For example, the legendary Arnold Palmer, a phenomenal putter in his day, was always easily indentifiable by his exaggerated knock-kneed stance. It didn't look pretty, but it worked.

Another putting legend was four times Open winner Bobby Locke. He too had a unique style. Rather than draw the putter blade straight back from the ball, he would sweep it back sharply on the 'inside' in a manner very similar to his actual golf swing. He always returned the putter blade on line at impact and was one of the best putters in the game.

Players of today are just as individualistic. Some even have to cope with a dreaded putting disease called 'the yips', a nervous reaction which affects the muscles of the hands. It can sometimes become a total and devastating affliction. Former Masters champion Bernhard Langer has had several bouts of the 'yips'. He has tried several different methods to find a cure and continues to experiment in an attempt to defeat the affliction. Figs 76 and 77 show two of his variations, whilst Ryder Cup star Sam Torrance supports an extra-long putter under his chin . . . And it works!

Fig 77 . . . and he is currently putting well with this unique variation!

Fig 78 Sam Torrance demonstrates his extra-long putter.

The Stance

This should be easy and comfortable, similar to your golf swing set-up, only a little less complicated.

Simply stand with your feet comfortably apart, bend from the waist and flex your knees. This should feel solid yet comfortable and still allow room for your arms to swing freely from your shoulders.

The Arms

Keep your left elbow towards the target and maintain this throughout the stroke. The right arm should fall in softly and without tension towards your right hip bone.

> **STAR TIP**
> *When putting, maintain the triangle of the shoulders and the arms.*
>   Maria Olazabal

I like to think of the left arm as being the swinging or controlling arm during the putting stroke. Turning it slightly outwards, but with the back of the hand facing directly towards the target, firms up the muscles of the forearm and wrist. Your hand, wrist, forearm and upper arm should now be capable of swinging as one unit.

The right arm is the 'pusher' or touch arm in the putting stroke. In a relaxed position, with the elbow resting lightly against or just away from your right hip bone, the right shoulder remains passive.

The Grip

Most of the good putters hold the putter very lightly. A good test is to rest the putter blade on the grass and to open your fingers sufficiently to reduce all pressure. Then re-grip with sufficent tightness to allow the weight of the club to be lifted gently from the ground.

You want a grip that lets your hands work in total unison, just as they should in the golf swing itself. I recommend the basic

Figs 79 (a)–(c)   The basic putting stance.

Fig 79 (a)   The stance.

Fig 79 (b)   The left arm is the 'swinger', with the elbow towards the target line.

Fig 79 (c)   The right arm is the 'pusher'.

reverse overlap. This is the most popular grip and has many variation. Here, I will only outline the basics; you will have plenty of time to experiment with variations at a later date.

> **KEY POINT**
> When putting, both hands should feel alive and sensitive on the club.

The Basic Reverse Overlap

The ball should be placed just inside the left heel and your head should be positioned directly over it or behind the line. Drop a ball away from your eye line in order to test.

1. Place the palms of your hands on either side of the putter grip so that the palms are facing one another and the right hand is just below the left. Make sure they are at right angles to your intended line.
2. Wrap the fingers of your right hand around the grip so that the right thumb is pointing directly down the shaft.
3. Close your left hand around the putter handle, again making sure that you point the thumb down the shaft.
4. To complete the reverse overlap grip, allow the index finger of your left hand to

Figs 80 (a)–(d)   The basic reverse overlap.

Fig 80 (a)   Eye line test. The ball should land on top or just behind.

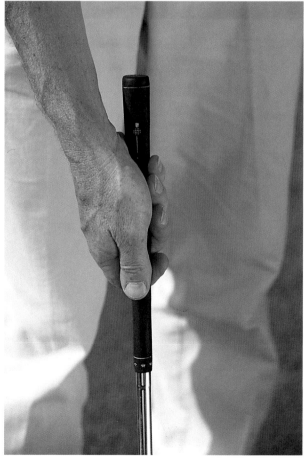

Fig 80 (b)   First, position your right hand with the thumb on top.

rest on the last two or three fingers of your right hand, either curled around the knuckles or extended down over the fingers of the right hand, whichever is most comfortable.

This will have the effect of restricting wrist action during and after impact, which is an important element in putting technique.

5. Make sure that your thumbs are pointing down the shaft (*see* Fig 80(c)).

The Stroke

As stated, the left arm is the swinger, the right hand the pusher. However, the right hand only delivers push or power just prior to impact.

The movement should hinge from the shoulders, using an action similar to that of a pendulum, with the same unhurried smoothness. This will create a perfect arc at the base of your swing. You should

sense that your left arm more than your right controls the motion, yet both arms are still working as one unit.

A good image to keep is to think in terms of *left arm control – right hand*

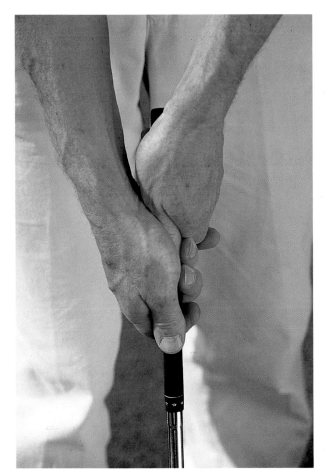

Fig 80 (c)   Then, add your left hand with the thumb pointing directly down the shaft.

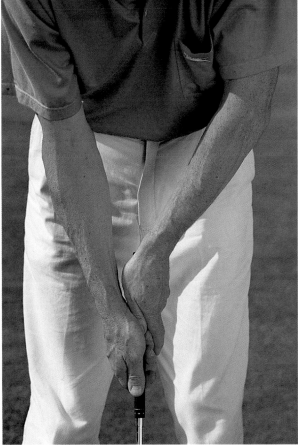

Fig 80 (d)   Note how the index finger of your left hand should be positioned. This can vary, however.

Fig 81   Accelerate the putter head.

Fig 82   Imagine you are holding a snooker cue on line until the putt drops.

strength. Your backswing must be shorter than your through-swing to achieve this goal. So, also think in terms of *short back* and *long through*.

As a beginner, you will be surprised at how little strength is required to set the ball rolling. Your initial inclination will be to take the putter head back too far and then to decelerate as you approach the ball. This leads to inconsistency.

KEY POINT
Always accelerate the putter head through the ball at and after the impact.

To get the idea of accelerating the clubhead at impact practise the following two-stage exercise.

Practice Exercise

Stage One   Line-up three or four balls just inside the left heel. Place the putter blade behind the first ball and without taking a backswing accelerate the head of the putter towards the target. If you are not doing this exercise correctly two things will happen:

1. The putter head will screw off line.
2. You will hit the ball twice because you did not accelerate the putter head quickly enough.

Repeat the exercise with each ball until you can achieve instant acceleration with accuracy.

Stage Two   Place a small object, say a tee peg, 2 or 3in (5 or 8cm) behind the ball. Line the putt up as before, but this time bring the putter blade back no further than the peg and again practise your acceleration.

Another good tip is to take a pointer from the world of snooker. If you have ever watched Steve Davis, you will have noticed how he holds the cue through on line after each pot. It will pay you to do the same with the putter head. In other words, stop and hold the putter head still for a few moments at the completion of your smooth, accelerated stroke. Even wait for the 'death rattle' – the sound of the ball dropping into the cup. In this way, you will ensure that you have kept your head perfectly still and increase your chances of

Figs 83 (a) and (b)   Use a tee peg to restrict your backswing.   (b)

maintaining a positive attitude to your putting.

Finally, if you have watched world class putters, you will have noticed how they stick to a set routine. You, too, should develop a pre-putt routine. Here's one that you can use.

The Pre-Putt Routine

Let us assume you have assessed the line and are ready to putt. Look at the target and then take two short practice swings to get a feel for the distance and the strength needed to get the ball to the hole. Now,

---

KEY POINT
Do not change your mind once you have had a look and taken your practice strokes.

---

immediately place the putter head behind the ball, take one more glance at the hole or line and putt without delay.

Reading Greens

There are some superb books on the market dealing with the subject. Read them when you have played a few

different courses and putted on greens of various characters.

However, you should not fall into the trap of over-reading the green before you know what you are looking for. You will begin to see things that are not there, placing doubts in your mind. Worst of all, you may develop another cause of slow play, imitating the prolonged routines of touring pros who study greens at length. Remember, their livelihood depends on it; they also know what they are looking for.

Useful Advice

Here is some overall advice concerning the most accurate way to read a green.

> **RULES CHECK**
> Never touch any part of the 'line' to the hole.

1. Look at the surrounding area and assess the general contours as you approach the green. These first impressions will invariably be the correct ones.
2. Once on the green, concentrate your attention on the area near the cup. This is where the ball should be slowing down and thus take any slight borrows.

> **KEY POINT**
> It is far easier to sink a putt uphill than downhill.

3. Aim at the back of the hole on most putts and try not to leave the ball short. 'Never up, never in' is a well-known golfing cliché, and a good one.
4. Always try to leave your holing-out putt *below* the cup on a sloping green.
5. Always be positive and remember to accelerate the putter head on short putts. Even if you do miss a few this way and have to face some tricky four-footers coming back, it is still best to maintain a positive attitude.

> **RULES CHECK**
> When attending the flag, never let the ball hit the stick.

One final putting tip. When playing on seaside courses – known as links – most greens are usually quite flat. This makes it difficult to read subtle borrows and slopes. It pays to remember the old adage which states that all greens slope to the sea. Obviously, this cannot be the case all the time, but it is astonishing how many times this works in practice. However, a short putt struck firmly to the back of the hole will always hold its line – no matter what the condition of the local tide!

Fig 84   *Peter Senior's long-handled putter is simply propped under the chin, with the right hand used to initiate the pendulum-type stroke.*

Putting Model Review

1. Maintain a comfortable address position, keeping the head and body still.
2. Allow room for the arms to swing and grip lightly.
3. Play the ball off the left heel, and hold your head over or behind ball.
4. Accelerate the clubhead towards hole or intended line and hold it.
5. Develop a routine.

> **KEY POINT**
> The key to putting is to keep the body and head absolutely still while allowing the hands and arms to control the strike.

6. Putt to the back of the hole and be positive – 'never up never in'.
7. Do not over-read greens.
8. Do not change your mind.
9. All greens slope to the sea!

CHAPTER 17

AWKWARD LIES

Unfortunately, you will find that not all golf courses are flat and the way to the green is not always straightforward. This can prove a problem when you have built a correctly-grooved swing on the *flat* surfaces of the practice area. You are suddenly forced to take an extra factor on board. However, being able to cope and consequently score when faced with these problems on the course is what makes a supreme golfer.

As one famous teacher once said, 'I can teach you how to swing a golf club, but I can't make you into a golfer'. How true this is. The ability to manufacture shots, to get the ball onto the green from any lie and from any situation is the making of a master golfer.

A touring professional's livelihood is determined by his ability to get 'up and down', and by his ability to turn three shots into two. A beginner can never expect to be in that league. There is simply not enough time in his cluttered day. However, by acquiring a consistent swing shape, you can expect more success than most because your technique will give you more control to play from those awkward lies.

> **KIT CHECK**
> Spiked golf shoes help you to keep a firm stance.

Ball Below Feet

The first thing you should realize is that the ball always reacts to the slope. Thus, the ball will slice when it is below your feet, so aim left of the target.

With the ball below you, you will be automatically forced into using a more upright swing because that is the only way you will make contact with the ball.

Fig 85   Ball below feet requires a steep swing.

Figs 86 (a) and (b)   The set-up for ball below feet.

Fig 86 (a)   Sit well back on the heels and flex the knees.

Fig 86 (b)   Swing in a much steeper plane.

Automatically, you will lean forward with the slope; so get your weight back on your heels, bend your knees and use the full length of the grip to compensate. Test your balance and practise your backswing path a few times to familiarize yourself with the new feel.

Make no attempt to be too 'text-book' with your swing. As with all specialist shots, you will be relying mainly on your ability to swing your arms freely and to use your hands. (This is why golfers with too much body action have so much difficulty playing special situation shots.)

So once again, your free-arm method will stand you in good stead.

KEY POINT

Ball below – sure to slice.
Ball above – sure to hook.
Uphill lie – adds loft to your club.
Downhill lie – de-lofts your club.

Once you have got the feeling of your upright swing path, settle yourself and place the club head behind the ball, then concentrate on a smooth swing. Any attempt to force this shot will result in a loss of balance.

Obviously, you should not attempt the miraculous and use a wood in this type of situation. Play a conservative iron and preserve your score.

Many cards have been ruined by going for distance in this situation.

Figs 87 (a) and (b)   The set-up for ball above feet.

Fig 87   Weight forward – choke down the grip for control.

Fig 87 (b)   Swing on a much flatter plane when the ball is above feet.

Ball Above Feet

The flight of the ball will move left to right on this shot, so aim to the right of target.

It helps if you can visualize playing baseball or rounders because you will be called on to use a 'flat' swing plane because of the position of the ball above your feet.

Set up with your weight towards your toes, choke down on the grip for more control and play the ball back in your stance.

Before playing the shot, practise your flat swing plane using the hands and arms and turning your shoulders. As with the ball below your feet, do not try to swing too hard or you could mishit the ball.

Allow your right side to follow through as you strike the ball. The result will be a low-hooking flight, so allow for a lot of run when the ball lands.

This means that you will be denied the option of flighting the ball high. So, do not expect it to stop on the green as a normal shot would. There is also a tendency for

KEY POINT

Balance is imperative for good and consistent shot making. Forcing shots will only cause the shoulders to overreact with disastrous results. An off-balance swing will bring off-line results.

So, stay balanced – and stay straight!

the blade to spin 'open', so in these circumstances a firm grip is essential.

Uphill Lie

Such a lie adds loft to any club you use. This means that a five iron might well give you a seven-iron flight. In other words, the ball will fly higher, which in turn means a loss of distance. Use a less lofted club than you normally would take for the distance.

Set yourself up with more weight on your right foot and try to align your shoulders to the slope. Play the ball more forward in your stance.

These adjustments are made because you intend to make the clubhead follow the contour of the hill. You are going to sweep the ball up the hill.

Because your weight is already on your right leg, you must not attempt to put more on it when you make your turn. Try to lean into the hill on the downswing, and keep the club and your body moving up the slope.

Always take much more club than you

Fig 88   The stance for an uphill lie.

Figs 89 (a)–(d)   Uphill lie sequence.

Fig 89 (a)   The club approaches.

Fig 89 (b)   Keep the club head moving . . .

think necessary. You will get very little roll from uphill shots.

Downhill Lie

The ball will always fly lower on this shot because the slope de-lofts the clubface. So, choose a club with more loft to put height and 'carry' on the ball.

Set yourself up with your weight towards your left leg, angle your shoulders to the slope and position the ball back in your stance.

Take care to stay balanced when you make your turn. On the downswing, let the clubhead and your right side follow the slope of the hill. You can embellish the shot by letting your right leg 'go walkies' after the ball. This was a trick used by the old maestro Henry Cotton.

This is not an attempt to introduce gimmickry to your game, it is just one of those delightful variations to encourage you to improvise when faced with an awkward shot.

Fig 90   Stance for the downhill shot.

Fig 89 (c)   . . . up the slope . . .

Fig 89 (d)   . . . to a good follow through.

Figs 91 (a)–(h)   Downhill sequence.

Fig 91 (a)   As you start back keep a solid base.

Fig 91 (b)   Half way back . . .

Fig 91 (e)   . . . start down with the arms, keep the left leg
solidly braced. The right knee begins to fold.

Fig 91 (f)   Impact! Let the clubhead follow the slope.

Fig 91 (c)   . . . nearly there, and still balanced.

Fig 91 (d)   At the top . . .

Fig 91 (g)   If the slope is steep, let the right leg go.

Fig 91 (h)   Walkies!

Working the Ball

If you have a good clubline through the ball, you will hit the ball straight. You will also have no difficulty bending it at will.

Let us start with the easiest of all, and one of the easiest to achieve.

The Fade

I term the fade a 'classy' slice because the ball starts left of the target as per a slice, but fades gently to the right at the end of its flight.

Use your normal set-up, aligning your body and clubface in the exact direction that you want the ball to finish. Now, simply turn your whole body so that it is pointing to the left of the target, making sure that the clubface is still pointing in the direction where you want the ball to end up.

Then, all you do is make your usual swing. However, remember that the more you face to the left, the more the ball turns right. The relationship of the body to the line of flight will cause you to automatically cut across the ball, producing left-to-right flight.

This also drastically reduces distance and should be taken into account. For example, play a five iron instead of a six.

The Draw

Simply reverse the above procedure for this most coveted type of flight. Adopt your usual set-up, aligning the face of the club directly at your target. Next, turn your body to the right but do not alter the alignment of the clubface.

Concentrate on simply swinging the club as per normal. The swing path will be in-to-out in relation to the line of flight. The ball will start right of the target with sidespin, causing it to 'draw' back, or hook, to the left.

To increase the amount of draw, turn your body to the right. Allow also for

Fig 92   The set-up for the fade.

Fig 93   The set-up for the draw shot.

more run on the ball by using a more lofted iron than usual, say a six instead of a five.

A Special Note on Club Selection

It is far easier to fade (slice) with longer irons (the five, four and three). On the other hand, the more lofted the club, the more backspin you produce, and backspin always counteracts sidespin.

The opposite is the case for draw. You will in effect be closing or de-lofting the club; therefore, if you de-loft a no. 3 iron, you are going to get very little height on the ball.

This often foils the handicapper's anti-slice gimmick of hooding the face at address. This ploy is effective up to a no. 5 iron, but then lack of loft on the long irons makes it impossible to get the ball airborne.

High and Low shots

The easiest way to vary the trajectory of your shots is to change the position of the ball in your stance. This is one of the rare circumstances when you should do this.

> **KEY POINT**
> Think ball-forward-and-a-full-finish for a high shot, and ball-back, brief-finish for a low shot.

For the high-flying shot, move the ball forward in your stance. If your swing action is good, you will strike the ball with a more upward blow. You will be striking the ball at the very limit of your swing base and have less margin for error. To be effective, ensure good leg action and complete your finish. Be positive on this shot for the best results.

To keep the ball low, you must adopt a similar technique to chipping. In other words, keep your hands forward and the ball in the middle of your stance, with the weight shaded toward your left foot. This set-up will ensure that you de-loft the clubface. Keep your finish brief and crisp. Moving the ball back in the stance and placing the weight more on the left side

Fig 94   For the high shot, move the ball towards the left heel, stance open.

Fig 95   The set-up for a low shot; keep hands forward throughout your swing.

will cause you to strike down sharply into the ball, increasing backspin. It is a good shot to cheat the wind.

Proof that such shots work was displayed by Arnold Palmer, who had the courage to manufacture an 'under-wind' shot by deliberately half-topping his no. I iron for long fairway shots. These deliberate mishits did not look good, but they were highly effective. I should add that ground conditions must be just right for this type of shot. Palmer was playing on the hard-baked fairways of a seaside course. Such a shot would not work on a 'spongy' parkland layout!

CHAPTER 18

GETTING OUT OF TROUBLE

Here are some escape route techniques which will stand you in good stead when you miss the fairway.

Sand

A sandtrap, in many instances, can be a haven. Indeed, most professionals prefer a greenside bunker shot to a chip because, for them, it is an easy shot. They have spent many hours perfecting their sand techniques.

Bobby Locke, who won four Opens, was a brilliant bunker player and well he deserved to be. He would practise for hours on end, and never stopped until he actually holed one.

> **RULES CHECK**
> Never ground your club in a sand trap or bunker.

You haven't time for that sort of devotion, neither have you ready access to a practice bunker. The only practice most weekend players get is when they get in the bunker on the course. So, somewhere on the green will do at first, but get it *out* you must! Here is how. These instructions apply when the ball is lying reasonably well in the trap, in other words your average greenside bunker shot.

Stage One Line up your shot before you get into the bunker by checking your escape route to the flag. Sometimes, when you get down into the bunker, your view is hampered by the lip of the trap. When

Fig 96   Greenside bunker shot. Face left of target, but keep the blade 'open' and above the sand.

you step into sand allow your feet to judge its texture.

Your set-up is similar to a pitch shot, except that you should open your stance somewhat more and remember to hold the clubhead so that everything is facing left except the blade of the club.

The effect of this manoeuvre will be to 'open' the blade, or to lay it back. Now weaken your grip by turning your right hand to the left, so that it is more on top of the handle of the club. This takes the power from your right hand and helps to prevent the blade closing at impact. As you adjust your feet, wiggle your shoes into the sand for a firm footing. You are now ready to swing.

Stage Two   Your swing path on the downswing will follow your shoulder line to the left, but the ball will go straight towards the target. On landing, it will spin to the right because of the out-to-in swing path.

KEY POINT
Your mental picture is of the clubhead sliding under the ball from a point about 2in (50cm) behind, to a spot well ahead of it. When you take your swing, make sure you complete each part of your action. Do not jab or quit, but swing through.

Figs 97 (a)–(e)   The bunker.

Fig 97 (a)   When playing from a bunker, make sure you complete your backswing.

Fig 97 (b)   On the downswing, aim at a spot about 2in (10cm) behind the ball.

Finally, resist the temptation to have a manic hack at the ball. Instead, develop a smooth, accelerating rhythm.

Judging how hard or how long your backswing should be to produce your shot is controlled by your intent, and will come with time and practice.

Greenside Bunker Shot Review

1. Assess your line before you get into the trap.

2. Point the leading edge of the club at the target.
3. Open your stance, which will also lay back your blade.
4. Visualize cutting under the ball.
5. Aim at a spot 2in (50cm) behind the ball.
6. Swing through the sand, following your shoulder line. Keep the blade open.

Awkward Sand Shots

Unfortunately, the ball does not always

stop conveniently in a good lie in the centre of the sandtrap. So here is how you excavate the ball from some of the most awkward resting places.

Ball Under the Lip

Set yourself with your weight on your right foot and take a solid stance. Aim at a spot just behind the ball and hit *hard*, up and under. Do not go for any heroics. Nobody can expect to be accurate in those situations. Just be content to get it out. If you fall back after the shot, do not

Fig 97 (c)   A cushion of sand will lift the ball as you cut underneath it . . .

Fig 97 (d)   . . . and send it towards the target.

Fig 97 (e)   Always complete your finish.

Figs 98 (a)–(j)   Ball under lip.

Fig 98 (a)   From a solid stance . . .

Fig 98 (e)   . . . an up and under!

Fig 98 (f)   The ball comes out . . .

Fig 98 (g)   . . . after which . . .

Fig 98 (b) ... the club starts back ...

Fig 98 (c) ... but the body turn is curtailed by the awkward stance.

Fig 98 (d) The clubhead approaches – ready to give the ball ...

Fig 98 (h) ... you can ...

Fig 98 (i) ... let yourself ...

Fig 98 (j) ... go!

worry. Just keep that clubhead moving up and under.

Ball in a Buried Lie or Foot Print

Sometimes, you can see only the top of the ball when it is in the bunker. Do not attempt the standard bunker shot for this one. Instead, play this shot with the ball further back in your stance. Lift the club up steeply and chop the leading edge into

the sand. This also applies to the 'poached egg' lie.

Do not expect to follow through because the clubhead has been travelling steeply downwards. The ball will come out lower than usual with no backspin, so expect it to roll.

The Cut-Up Shot

You will have to try this shot if you land in a bunker with an exceptionally high lip. It is

Fig 100   'The poached egg' lie. Play the same as a buried lie.

similar to the standard bunker shot, except that you must open your stance further and lay your blade back more. Swing across the line of your shoulders and good luck! If you do not fancy your chances with this one, bite the bullet and go out sideways.

The Long Bunker Shot

Play this shot with a less open stance and position the ball mid-way between the feet. Choose a pitching wedge instead of a sand iron, and concentrate on taking a minimum amount of sand.

> **STAR TIP**
> *When the ball is higher or lower than your stance, position your hands by sliding them up or down the grip.*
> Maria Olazabal

Play a full swing and ensure that you complete your follow-through. Do not try to force the shot. Make it your priority to strike the exact spot in the sand at which you are aiming.

There are of course, many other situations which will present themselves in actual play. The basic technique described will allow you, with experience, to work them out for yourself.

Fig 99   A buried lie in a bunker. Play the ball further back in your stance.

Figs 101 (a)–(d) The long bunker shot.

Fig 101 (a) Use a pitching wedge and play the ball midway between the feet.

Fig 101 (b) Play a full swing.

Fig 101 (c) Take the minimum amount of sand . . .

Fig 101 (d) . . . and move right through to your finish.

Fig 102   An 'explosion' for a long bunker shot.

Deep Rough

Your first priority in the rough is to look for the shortest route out. Under no circumstances should you try for distance: it cannot happen. Your second one is to assess your lie realistically. If you hear yourself saying 'no way', forget the bravado, drop out and take a penalty stroke.

Do not try to improve your lie by laying the grass back with your foot to get at the ball. This is one of the commonest forms of cheating among weekend golfers. Do not be tempted!

Finally, pick your sand iron for the job if you decide it is worth the risk to try to play the ball out. Position the ball well back in your stance and keep your hands forward. You are now going to attempt to pick the clubhead up steeply and hit down almost vertically just behind the ball. With luck, the ball will pop out, but it will not go very far nor necessarily straight. From an aesthetic point of view, this stroke is not a pretty sight, but it works!

Light Rough

This area is frequently found on the course, and causes the most aggravation to the handicapper because he is in it so often. Shots from this type of lie are always unpredictable, so be thankful for what you get.

Much depends on getting a good lie. If you can see the back of the ball, you have a fair chance of making an accurate short shot to the green. If you cannot get a shot at the back of the ball, then you must make some minor adjustments to your stance and your choice of club.

However, you must take into consideration that as the club descends on the ball, it is bound to compress some of the grass between the clubface and the ball (thus reducing friction by filling the grooves with squashed grass). Expect the ball to roll further on landing as a result. Depending on how long the grass is, you can expect the clubface to be forced to close a little at impact, causing a hook. So, aim slightly right of the target.

Play the ball further back in your stance and choose a club with more loft than you would normally use for the distance. This will ensure that you swing with more of a descending blow, thus getting less grass between the blade and the ball.

Rough and Light Rough Review

1. In heavy rough, play it back and have a hack!
2. From a good lie in light rough, allow for low flight and aim to the right.
3. From a bad lie in light rough, play the ball further back in your stance, take more loft and expect a hook and more roll.

PART 4

FITNESS FOR GOLF

CHAPTER 19

FITNESS

'Now you're retired, take up a little gentle golf', used to be the advice to retiring septuagenarians. Gentle golf? There's no such thing!

Most people over forty-five will find that their bodies are out of condition for golf. Even those who have kept fit by swimming or the occasional visit to the squash court discover that the former simply builds too much dead bulk around the shoulders while the latter ruins the wrist action. Some super-fit rugby players find it very hard turning from the waist and shoulders without their heads following too.

If you take your game really seriously you must find time to devote to a regular programme to free up your limbs and strengthen the parts that are specific to golf.

I have devised a course of priorities. The more you do in the order laid out, the better-equipped physically you will be for golf. Learn to do them – they will help to sustain your golf for life. (There is still time to learn them if you are over thirty, but you may well find it harder.)

Start at the top of the exercise schedule and do your best. You will be surprised how well your body will respond, provided that you take it easy at first.

Arms

The primary reason why the golf swing fails is because players have never developed an arm swing. Maintaining the ability to swing your arms, without assistance from your body, is the one key factor that can transform your golf. So learn to swing those arms!

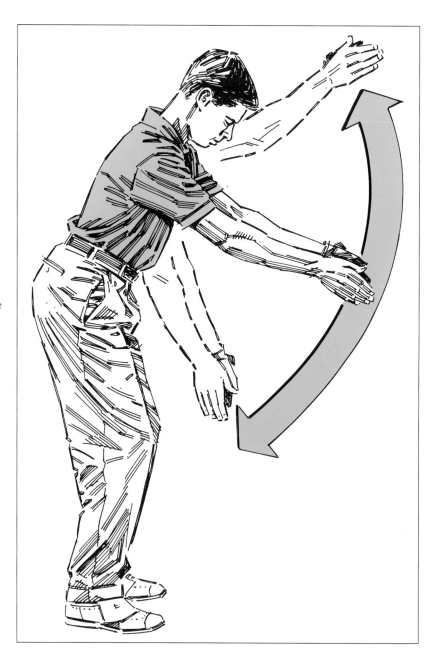

Fig 103   An invaluable arm- and shoulder-freeing exercise.

Practice Exercise

Take up your correct address position, minus a club, and let your arms hang down by your sides. Now swing your arms slowly and deliberately up to, or just beyond, your shoulders and down again without raising your body height or head.

Repeat this exercise for a few minutes each day. Do it as a warm-up before you play a round of golf. Repeat the exercise with a short iron as described in Chapter 6.

Hands

Unless your hands and wrists are strong and supple, you will not make the top grade. When taking up golf late in life, weak hands often cause the most problems, particularly for people who have never used their hands other than for pushing a pen or whose hands have been in constant use lifting or carrying.

For instance, a milkman's hands are under constant strain. The legacy of such an occupation is that the ligaments are stretched and become set, making some crucial wrist movements difficult, if not impossible.

For that very reason the great Open champion of the thirties, Walter Hagen, would lift neither his suitcase nor his golf bag in order to preserve his hands.

You should start right away to exercise your hands as follows:

Practice Exercise One

Place the hands together in a 'choir boy praying' position. Lift your elbows, forcing your palms to stay together. Work gently and rhythmically, levering your elbows up and down.

Practice Exercise Two

Assume the position set out above, only make a cage of your fingers. Spring your fingers in and out.

Practise Exercise Three

For finger strength and wrist flexibility, obtain a squash ball and squeeze it between finger and thumb. Repeat with every finger of both hands.

Fig 104   The choir boy exercise!

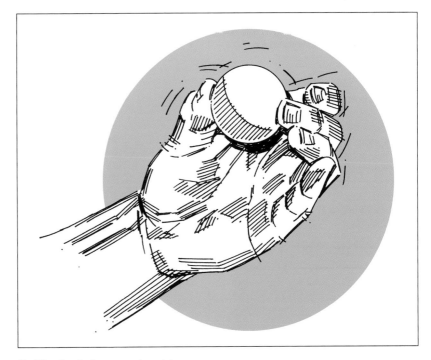

Fig 105   Get the fingers supple and strong.

Figs 106 (a) and (b)   Make good use of your old newspapers.

Grasp the squash ball and make a fist out of your hand. Rotate the wrist clockwise and anti-clockwise, as well as up and down. This is guaranteed to give you a firm handshake. Be careful not to over-do it though!

Practice Exercise Four

If you have ever wondered what to do with those old newspapers, place a good quantity on a table top, place your hand face down and quickly scrunch the pages into a small ball, working each one of those fingers as you do so.

Practice Exercise Five

Knock a nail into the middle of a broom handle and suspend a small weight on a string. Now wind it up on the fingers and down again. Done properly, this is agony, but well worth the pain.

Fig 107   Try this exercise to gain powerful fingers and forearms.

Back Muscles

The muscles of the average person's back never get exercised – these are the muscles in the small of the back on either side of the spine, and very hard to get at with standard exercises. However, here is an old standard routine which really does the trick.

Practice Exercise

Lie face down on a firm surface with your arms by your side. Lift your legs and pull up with your chest.

At first, you will only be able to repeat this exercise once or twice, but perseverance will pay handsome dividends and preserve your precious back.

Fig 108   Strengthen the back muscles.

Figs 109 (a) and (b)   Sit-ups are good for golf and good for the stomach.   (b)

Fig 110   Leg-ups also help to tone the stomach muscles.

Legs

Get cycling! By cycling, I really mean use an exercise bike. Your local leisure centre will have a convoy of them. A regular five-minute session is all you need to keep those legs strong and active for your eighteen holes.

Stomach

Even if you are of slim build, you will need to strengthen those stomach muscles. They support you at address and throughout your action. Sit-ups from various inclined angles will be most effective, as will a short session of leg-ups.

Take the time to do some of these targeted exercises, and you will be astonished at the difference a properly toned-up body will make to your golf.

CHAPTER 20

PRACTICE AND TUITION

All books sooner or later mention that dreaded word: 'practice'. Grit your teeth and plough through it. Failures don't practise, winners do!

The worst excuse a coach can hear is, 'I'm sorry, I haven't had time to practise'. One of the cleverest excuses, and one which the student thinks will placate his teacher is, 'I didn't practise in case I was doing it wrong'.

That simply will not wash! You must have the courage to go out and make you mistakes. By so doing and having them corrected, you will recognize your errors and rectify them.

STAR TIP
Funnily enough, the harder I practise, the luckier I get!
(Gary Player, on being lucky).

Make Time to Practise

Get up ten minutes earlier, or pop out into the garden when you get home from work for a few swings. You can find the time if you really want to. If you do not practise, you do not deserve to play well (and should not expect to!).

Make a resolution to pick up a club every day, even if it is just to hold it. Swing it if you have the space. If not, practise your grip and your stance, even some tiny chips on the carpet with a seven iron. Become familiar with your club's feel. You should become accustomed, intimate even, with its balance. You will thus avoid using too 'strangling' a grip.

In this book, you will also find special

KEY POINT
The key to practice is to form the habit of practising. Try to allot a specific time and a specific place for it. Once the habit has been formed and you begin to reap the benefits of your endeavour, you will find that practice is no longer a chore, it can even become a compulsive pleasure!

---

positional exercises that you can do with and without a club. *Do them.* As well as laying the foundation for more intense practice at a later stage, they constantly train your body to accept all the strange and awkward positions that, at first, seem not to be part of the proper golf swing.

If you are a born procrastinator, golf is not for you. More than likely you will be bitterly disappointed. You will need to possess inner strength and resolution to concentrate on learning.

A successful golfer must first and foremost have the desire and resolution to learn, and find the time to practise.

Taking Lessons

Take advice from only a qualified professional, one who will take time to teach and who will show interest in your progress.

It is rarely understood that *anyone* can set themselves up as a golf pro, just as a 'quack' doctor can. If in doubt, ask to see the person's PGA card.

Lessons from Friends

You will also be tempted to take instructions from your friends. *Don't!* It

doesn't matter that they are well intentioned; at best, you will pick up their faults; at worst, you will develop faults that may be incurable.

Let there be no doubt in your mind that teaching golf is now regarded as a highly skilled occupation. For example, the governing body of professionals, the PGA, does not allow its trainee pros to teach solo until their third year, even though they are already competent players (5 handicap or better golfers).

What about the expense? You cannot buy competence. In contrast to the price of clubs today, you could get ten private lessons for as little as £75, whereas you cannot buy one top-class metal wood for that!

A word of advice, though: do not be surprised if your tutor has his own theories and variations as attitudes and beliefs have changed through the years. In the fifties, it was Hogan's theory, then came 'square-to-square'. Cotton had a run for a while then it was Mr X, then Nicklaus.

There is always the latest fad or guru offering the 'true' golf swing in easy-to-swallow potions. At the time of writing, David Leadbetter is the most prominent theorist.

Never Attempt to Harness Your Swing

I do not recommend harnesses, special clubs, or other swing appliances that take over your body like a life-support machine, or any other gimmick in your search for a golf swing. They may occasionally be endorsed by a great player but they have never produced one!

My advice is let your own body teach you, not a contraption.

A BRIEF GLOSSARY OF
GOLF SWING TERMS

Clubface
At address: Shut (*see* Fig 111). Open (*see* Fig 112). Square (*see* Fig 113).
At the top: Shut (*see* Fig 114). Open (*see* Fig 115). Square (*see* Fig 116).

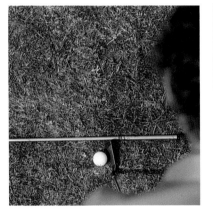

Fig 111   Clubface shut – turned to the left.

Fig 112   Clubface open – turned to the right.

Fig 113   Clubface square – leading edge facing directly to target.

Fig 114   Face of club shut.

Fig 115   Face of club open.

Fig 116   Square clubface.

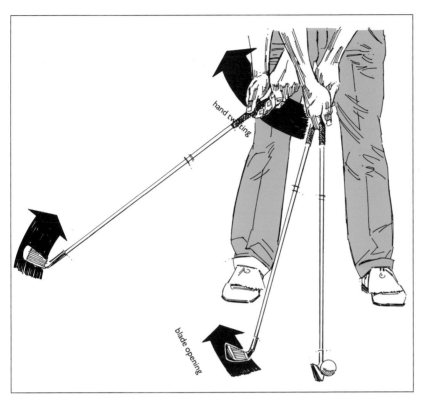

Fig 117 Clubface 'opening'.

Cross line at top The clubhead points to the right of target (*see* page 48).
'Fanning' 'Opening' the clubface on takeaway (*see* Fig 117).

Fig 118 Hands too high.

Fig 119 Hands too low.

Hands
  Forward: Hands ahead of clubhead at address (*see* page 38).
  Too high: No angle between wrists and shaft (*see* Fig 118).
  Too low: Angle between wrists and shaft too great (*see* Fig 119).

Off the heel   The ball is struck with the heel of the club (*see* Fig 120).
Off the toe   The ball is struck with the toe of the clubhead (*see* Fig 121).

Fig 120   *Off the heel (or socket, or shank).*

Fig 121   *Off the toe.*

Out of line   Takeaway fault. The clubhead is taken back 'outside' the correct line (*see* Fig 122).
Over laid-off   The clubhead points to the left of target (*see* page 32).
Over the top   The club comes 'forward', out of plane from the top of the swing.

Fig 122   *'Outside' the line.*

Shot

'Fat': The club hits the ground just behind the ball (*see* Fig 123).

'Thin': The ball is struck with the leading edge of the club (*see* Fig 124).

'Topped': The ball is struck a glancing blow on the top, knocking it along the ground (*see* Fig 125).

Stance   Your address position.

Closed: Right foot pulled back.

Open: Left foot pulled back.

Too wide: The feet are too far apart.

Too narrow: The feet are too close together.

Square: Feet, shoulders and blade are at right angles to the line of flight.

Fig 124   The ball is struck by the leading edge of the club.

Fig 123   Hitting behind the ball.

Fig 125   A 'topped' shot.

Fig 126   Too much on the inside.

Too much on the inside   Takeaway fault.
The clubhead is taken back 'inside' the
correct line.

GLOSSARY

Address   The position the player takes at the ball prior to making the swing.

Air shot   A complete miss.

Albatross   A score of 3 under par – either holing in one at a par 4 or in two at a par 5.

Angle of attack   The angle at which the clubhead approaches the ball on the forward swing.

Approach shots   Shots to a green from about 150yd (137m) inwards.

Apron   The grassy area surrounding the green which is normally cut to a length slightly shorter than the fairway, but slightly longer than the green.

Balata   Thin cover on top-quality golf balls.

Better-ball match   A match in which two players play against another two players, and only the better score of each side counts.

Birdie   A score of one stroke under par on a hole.

Blind hole   A hole where the player cannot see the green or the flagstick when playing an approach shot.

Bogey   One stroke over par on a hole.

Borrow   The amount a player should allow for a putt to move sidewards on a sideslope.

Carbon-fibre   One of the new materials used for golf club shafts instead of steel.

SCORING CHART		
Par	Score	
5	5	= Par
5	4	= Birdie
5	3	= Eagle
5	6	= Bogey
5	7	= Double Bogey
5	8	= Triple Bogey
4	4	= Par
4	3	= Birdie
4	2	= Eagle
4	5	= Bogey
3	3	= Par
3	2	= Birdie
3	1	= Eagle, or a hole in one!
3	4	= Bogey

Carry   The length which the ball travels from where it is struck to where it lands.

Casual Water   Any accumulation of rain or flood water on the course.

Chip shot   A low running approach shot.

Choke Down   Hold the club further down the grip.

Close lie   A ball lying tight to the ground' surface.

Closed alignment   The left side of the body closer to the ball-to-target line than the right side.

Closed face   Clubface aimed left of the correct position either at the address or during the actual swing.

Clubface   The striking surface of the club.

Course rating   The score a scratch golfer should make when playing well under

normal conditions. Also known as SSS (Standard Scratch Score).

Cup   The lining inside the hole, normally made of metal or plastic.

Divot   A piece of turf removed by the club-head when swinging.

Dormie   Where a player or side is ahead during a match by as many holes as remain to be played.

Double bogey   Two strokes over par on a hole.

Down   The number of holes a player or side is behind during a match.

Draw   A ball curving slightly from right to left through the air.

Drive   Shot made with a driver (no. 1 wood) when playing from the teeing ground.

Dropping   Where a golf ball may be lifted from an unplayable situation and dropped in another position. When dropping, the player must stand erect, facing his target, and drop the ball from shoulder-height at arm's length.

Duck hook   A shot that curves violently to the left with very little height on it.

Eagle   A hole played in two strokes under par.

Fade   A shot that moves slightly from left to right through the air.

Fairway   The area between the teeing ground and the green, which is regularly mown.

Flagstick   The marker in the hole on the green.

Follow-through   The part of the swing which occurs after impact.

Fourball   A match in which two players play their better ball against the better ball of another two players.

Foursome   A match in which two players play against another two players, each side using one ball and playing alternate shots.

Front nine   The first nine holes of a course.

Golf Foundation   Non-profit making entity which encourages junior golf by arranging group coaching for youngsters and staging national and international events.

Green   The closely mown area on which the hole is cut.

Grip   The material on the shaft on to which the player places his hands.

Grooves   Indentations cut into the face of iron clubs to impart backspin.

Gross score   The player's score for a round with no handicap deduction.

Ground under repair   Any area of a golf course which is being treated or repaired – often marked 'GUR'.

Halve   To complete a hole in the same score as the opposition in match-play.

Handicap   An adjustable figure awarded to players according to their scoring ability against the standard scratch score of a course.

Hazards   Natural or man-made areas filled with sand or water, in which the club cannot be grounded when addressing the ball.

Hooded   The position of the clubface if it is turned in to aim left of the target.

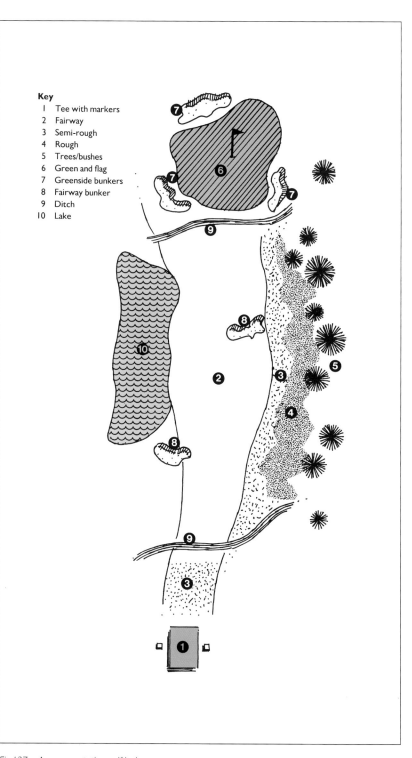

Key
1   Tee with markers
2   Fairway
3   Semi-rough
4   Rough
5   Trees/bushes
6   Green and flag
7   Greenside bunkers
8   Fairway bunker
9   Ditch
10 Lake

Fig 127   A representative golf hole.

Hook A shot which curves violently from right to left.

Inside-out The clubhead travelling from inside the ball-to-target line to outside it through the impact zone.

Lie The angle formed by the shaft and the sole of the club. Also used to describe the ball's position.

Loft The effective angle of the clubface as it hits the ball.

Match-play Where the result is decided by holes with match-play rules being applied.

Medal Play Where the player's score is recorded at each hole and totalled up at the end of the round, also known as stroke play.

Open face Clubface looking to the right of the target at address or impact. Also used to describe the face position in relation to the swing arc during the swing.

Open stance Where the right foot is closer to the ball-to-target line than the left at address.

Outside-in The clubhead travelling from outside to inside the ball-to-target line through impact.

Par The score a first-class player is expected to achieve on a hole allowing two putts on the green.

Pitch A high approach shot made with a nine iron, pitching wedge or sand wedge.

Pitchmark Indentation in the surface of the green caused by the ball on landing.

Plugged Ball A ball which remains in its own indentation when landing on soft ground.

Preferred lies Where players are allowed to place the ball on the fairways during the winter months or when the fairways are in poor condition.

Pull A shot which travels straight through the air but to the left of the target. Caused by the club's swingpath being out-to-in.

Push The exact opposite of the pull. Caused by the club's swing path being in-to-out.

Rough Anywhere that is not maintained and cut as a tee, fairway, green or hazard.

Royal and Ancient Golf Club of St Andrews The club was founded in 1754, and eventually became responsible for the Rules of Golf. It runs the Open Championship.

Rub of the Green If a ball in motion is accidentally deflected or stopped by an outside agent (human, animal, or part of the natural terrain) it is regarded as rub of the green. No penalty is involved and the ball must be played as it lies.

Shaft flex The amount by which a shaft is designed to bend. Shafts can be obtained in different degrees of flexibility.

Shank A shot struck on the inside part of the hosel on an iron club, also known as a socket.

Slice A shot which swerves violently from left to right, caused by an out-to-in swing path with the clubface either straight or open at impact.

Sole The bottom part of the club.

Square stance When both feet are equidistant from the ball-to-target line; it is also important to ensure that the body lines agree with the line across the toes.

Stroke The act of swinging a club with the intention of striking the ball.

Surlyn Resilient material used for golf ball covers. Much tougher and more cut-resistant than Balata.

Swingweight A measurement used to match clubs to each other so that they feel the same when swung. Most golf shops have a swingweight machine for checking clubs.

Takeaway The start of the backswing.

Target line The line connecting the ball and the target.

Texas wedge An American expression describing a shot played with a putter from off the green.

Through the green The area between the tee and the green, excepting hazards.

Topped shot When the bottom front edge of the clubface contacts the ball above its equator.

Two-Piece The most popular ball used by club golfers throughout the world. It is a solid piece of resilient material with a cover.

Vardon grip Named after the famous player Harry Vardon who popularized the overlapping grip.

APPENDIX

Useful Addresses

United Kingdom

Golf Foundation
Dir Miss Lesley Attwood
57 London Road
Enfield
Middlesex EN2 6DU
Tel: (081) 3674404

Golf Society of Great Britain
Mrs E J Drummond
Southview
Warren Road
Thurlestone
Devon TQ7 3NT
Tel: (0548) 560630

Hole in One Golf Society
Sec E W Parker
1 Vigilant Way
Gravesend
Kent
Tel: (0474) 534298

Ladies' Golf Union
Administrator Mrs Alma Robertson
The Scores
St Andrews
Fife KY16 9AT
Tel: (0334) 75811

The Professional Golfers' Association
Exec Dir J Lindsey
National Headquarters
Apollo House
The Belfry
Sutton Coldfield
West Midlands B76 9PT
Tel: (0675) 70333
Fax: (0675) 70674

Scottish Region
Sec Sandy Jones
Glenbervie Golf Club
Stirling Road
Larbert FK5 4SJ
Tel: (0324) 562541

Irish Region
Sec Michael McCumiskey
Dundalk Golf Club
Blackrock, Dundalk
Co Louth
Eire
Tel: (010 353) 4221193/7
Fax: (010 353) 4221899

Senior Golfers' Society
Sec Brigadier D Ross CBE
Milland Farmhouse
Liphook
Hampshire GU30 7PJ
Tel: (042 876) 200

England

English Golf Union
Sec K Wright
1–3 Upper King Street
Leicester LE1 6XF
Tel: (0553) 553042
Fax: (0533) 471322

English Ladies' Golf Association
Sec Mrs M J Carr
Edgbaston Golf Club
Church Road
Birmingham B15 3TB
Tel: (021) 4562088

Ireland

Irish Golf Union
Sec Ivan E R Dickson
Glencar House
81 Eglington Road
Donnybrook
Dublin 4
Tel: (0001) 694111

Irish Ladies' Golf Union
Sec Miss M P Turvey
1 Clonskeagh Road
Dublin 14
Tel: (0001) 696244

Scotland

Scottish Ladies' Golf Association
Sec Mrs L H Park
Chacewood
49 Fullarton Drive
Troon KA10 6LF
Tel: (0292) 313047

Wales

Welsh Golfing Union
Sec D G Lee
5 Park Place
Cardiff
South Glamorgan
Tel: (0222) 238467

Welsh Ladies' Golf Union
Hon Sec Miss P Roberts
Ysgoldy Gynt
Llanhennock
Newport
Gwent NP6 1LT
Tel: (0633) 420642

Overseas
America: USA and Canada

American Ladies' Professional Golf
Association
Commissioner Wiliam A Blue
2570 Volusia Avenue
Suite B
Daytona Beach
Florida 32114
Tel: (904) 254 8800
Fax: (904) 254 4755

American Professional Golfers' Associaton
Chief Exec Officer John J Rossi
Box 12458
100 Avenue of the Champions
Palm Beach Gardens
Florida 33418
Tel: (407) 624 8400

Canadian Ladies' Golf Association
Exec Dir Leonard Murphy
1600 James Naismith Drive
Gloucester
Ontario K1B 5N4
Tel: (613) 748 5642

Canadian Professional Golfers' Association
General Manager Robert H Noble
59 Berkeley Street
Toronto M5A 2W5
Tel: (416) 368 6104

United States Golf Association
Exec Dir David B Fay
USGA Golf House
Liberty Corner Road
Far Hills
New Jersey 07931
Tel: (201) 234 2300

Asia and Far East

Australian Golf Union
Japan Golf Association
Sec Gen Miss A Kato
606–6th Floor
Palace Building
Marunouchi
Chiyoda-ku
Tokyo
Tel: Tokyo (3) 571 0928

Australasia

Australian Golf Union
Sec C A Phillips
Golf Association House
155 Cecil Street
South Melbourne
Victoria 3205

Europe

European Golf Association
Gen Sec C Storjohann
En Ballègue
Case Postale CH–1066
Epalinges
Lausanne
Switzerland
Tel: (010) 41 21 7843532
Fax: (41 21) 7843536

INDEX